Autobiography in Ed

Publications Written or
Edited by Peter Abbs

English for Diversity

Autobiography in Education

The Black Rainbow
a symposium on the state of contemporary culture

Tract[1]
(a quarterly journal)

English Broadsheets
(sets of illustrated folders)
Introductory Series
First Series
Second Series

Approaches
(anthologies for young school leavers)
Into Action
Our World
Asking Questions
Creating for Ourselves

Stories for Today
(for adolescents with reading difficulties)
Ron's Fight
Ginger and Sharon
Frank's Fire
Linda's Journey
Joe and Carol
Diane's Sister
The Big Game
Rescue at Night
June's Work

[1] Gryphon Press, Brechfa, Llanon, Cardiganshire

Autobiography in Education

An introduction to the subjective discipline of
Autobiography and of its central place in the education of
teachers, with a selection of passages from a variety of
autobiographies, including those written by students

by Peter Abbs

HEINEMANN EDUCATIONAL BOOKS
LONDON

Heinemann Educational Books Ltd
LONDON   EDINBURGH   MELBOURNE   AUCKLAND
TORONTO   HONG KONG   SINGAPORE
KUALA LUMPUR   IBADAN   NAIROBI
JOHANNESBURG   LUSAKA   NEW DELHI

ISBN 0 435 80011 6 (cased edition)
ISBN 0 435 80012 4 (paperback edition)

Published by
Heinemann Educational Books Ltd
48 Charles Street, London W1X 8AH
Printed in Great Britain by
Morrison & Gibb Ltd, London and Edinburgh

Contents

Acknowledgements

I would like to acknowledge the support of Professor Jack L. Williams of the Education Department, University College of Wales, Aberystwyth, Miss Elizabeth Richardson, and Mr Tony Riding of the English Department, Hereford College of Education, who kindly made arrangements that enabled me to develop courses in Autobiography.

I would also like to thank all the students who took part in my Autobiography seminars for giving themselves to the work with such infectious enthusiasm and for allowing me to quote extracts from their writing.

The copyright passages are reprinted by kind permission of the following:

Penguin Books and Ronald Wilks for the extract from *My Childhood* by Maxim Gorki, translated by Ronald Wilks.

William Collins for the extract from *Memories, Dreams, Reflections* by Jung, ed. Jaffe, translated by Winston.

Secker & Warburg for the extract from *The Contrary Experience* by Herbert Read.

Faber & Faber for 'Child on Top of a Greenhouse' by Theodore Roethke from *The Collected Poems* and for extract from 'Burnt Norton' by T. S. Eliot from *Collected Poems 1909–1962*.

J. M. Dent and the Trustees for the Copyright of the late Dylan Thomas for 'Fern Hill' from *Collected Poems 1934–52*.

The Estate of the late Mrs Frieda Lawrence and Laurence Pollinger Ltd for 'Piano' by D. H. Lawrence from *The Collected Poems*.

For My Son Theodore

'Men go to gape at mountain peaks, at the boundless tides of the sea, the broad sweep of rivers, the encircling ocean and the motions of the stars; and yet they leave themselves unnoticed; they do not marvel at themselves.'

ST AUGUSTINE, *Confessions*

'The common cognomen of this world among the misguided and superstitious is "a vale of tears" from which we are to be redeemed by a certain arbitrary interposition of God and taken to Heaven – what a little circumscribed straightened notion! Call the world if you please the "vale of Soul-making". Then you will find out the use of the world . . . I say "Soul-making", Soul as distinguished from an Intelligence – There may be intelligences or sparks of the divinity in millions – but they are not souls till they acquire identities, till each one is personally itself.'

JOHN KEATS *in a letter to George and Georgiana Keats, 19 March 1819*

'I am an existentialist because I believe in the priority of the subject over the object, in the identity of the knowing subject and the existing subject; I am furthermore, an existentialist because I see the life of men and of the world torn by contraries, which must be faced and maintained in their tension, and which no intellectual system of a closed and complete totality, no immanentalism or optimism can resolve. I have always desired that philosophy should not be *about* something or somebody, but should be that very something or somebody, in other words, that it should be the revelation of the original nature and character of the subject itself.'

NICHOLAS BERDYAEV, *An Essay in Autobiography*

I Introduction

1. Establishing a Philosophical and Educational Base for the Discipline of Autobiography

In the past, it has been common practice for students on entering a College of Education or an Education Department at a University to be asked to reflect on their educational background as a personal preparation for the more impersonal studies of Psychology and Sociology which follow. I believe that such a practice harbours the seed of a great design, but that the conditions imposed by the timetable – two weeks in which to complete the memories and no time to collaboratively explore their implications and ramifications – have prevented the seed from germinating. As a result the practice has deteriorated to the level of another exercise. A moment's reflection about the intimate and creative nature of autobiography ought to tell us that such a momentous task cannot be properly tackled unless considerable time is allocated to it: and not only time, but also the possibility of extremely sensitive and tactful supervision. From my own experience with students writing their own autobiography, I would suggest that at least one term – with meetings every week, lasting a minimum of one hour, with groups not more than twelve in number – is essential if the project is to find its own particular shape and depth.

This in the busy framework of educational studies is a lengthy stretch of time. Many would consider it unjustified. If such a scheme in autobiography were being put forward at a staff-meeting, many would argue that any time allocated to such personal elusive activity would be better used by disseminating to the students more from the ever-expanding fund of empirical knowledge provided by the social sciences. Others would argue that the time would be more profitably spent by introducing the students to the practical problems of the classroom, to the hard realities of education. Both critics, for different reasons, would indicate that to develop a course in autobiography would be to digress too far from the pressing issues of modern education.

What then is the value of students, who are preparing to be teachers, devoting so much time to reflecting on the formative influences in their lives and considering, with imaginative sympathy, the formative influences on other lives? To begin to elaborate an adequate answer to this question, I must first answer the criticisms expressed above. It is important to notice that the two counter proposals, while different in content – one is academic, the other practical – have a common assumption. One group demands more knowledge: the other more technique: but both assume that education is an act of multiplication by which more and more is done or known. And behind this numerical notion lurks a further assumption: that education can successfully take place without reference to the condition of the individual. And this, sure enough, is the way in which education is still viewed in many of our schools, colleges and universities. Education, it is insisted, is a matter of ingesting information, of mastering technique. It is the notion of education that Dickens attacked in *Hard Times* and which F. R. Leavis pointed attention to when in his lecture *English – Unrest and Continuity* he quoted the following excerpt from a letter to *The Times*: 'University work falls into two main categories – contributions to knowledge and communicating knowledge to students.' The same conception of education has been given a respectable sociological form by, among others, John Vaizey:

> Modern education affects the economy in a number of ways: not only does it increase the flow of skills, but it assists people to acquire new techniques. Moreover it tends to destroy the traditional attitudes which so impede progress, and it links knowledge with methods of production.

In the industrial society, as the factory mass-produces products so the schools and institutions of education mass-produce knowledge and techniques. The individual is reduced to the status of a passive vessel moving on a conveyor belt and being filled, at the same time, with useful knowledge and necessary techniques. The result in our schools and colleges is a deep inertia among the students: a mindless torpor – or what might better be described as a pathology of boredom.

Given such a conception of the function of education it is exceedingly difficult to justify the work in autobiography I am advocating for colleges and departments of education. But, of course, it would be equally difficult to defend the place of drama, art, poetry, music, religion, myth – indeed all those subjective disciplines which seek to articulate the inner realm and to develop the whole man. Given such a solid empirical conception of education, all forms of imaginative enquiry, all forms of symbolic articulation, become 'soft options', indulgences, events doomed to live on the fringe of things.

We need then a different educational premise: a premise resting on actualities while it allows for flight into possibilities: a truer and more generous premise. In challenging the prevalent utilitarian dogma of education as the acquisition of facts and know-how, it might be helpful to ask, first of all, *where* does education take place? It would seem to take place inside the person. That seems obvious enough and I doubt such an observation would stir any controversy. It is the individual who knows, who reasons, who asks, who expresses, who seeks or fails to do so. There is, couching it in a different form, no knowledge, no science, no symbolism, no art, outside of all those individual minds which constitute, and have constituted, the human race. To end human life, which means to annihilate *all individual lives*, would be to end all education. This may appear to the reader obvious, even trite. Yet if we consider further the implication buried here, we may find ourselves moving towards a radically different conception of education from the one that is now so powerful. Indeed we may find ourselves coming very close to those interior truths and personal aspirations which, as I wish to show later, make the writing of autobiography so rich an enterprise.

Let us begin by restating the proposition that education takes place inside the person in the following way: *just as the act of creativity presupposes a creator, so knowledge presupposes a knower*. In their primary state, creation and knowledge are not objects-in-the-world, not artifacts which can be studied or measured or reproduced, but acts of the *individual* mind wholly engaged in articulating the import of a specific experience. I emphasize the word *individual* because the word *mind* suggests a pure domain unaffected by feelings or the drives of contingency, an unchanging palace of essences, but this we know, from the revelations of psycho-analysis and the arguments of existentialists, is not the case. Thought, in its primary state, is shot through with feeling and intentionality. Any study of the great philosophers reveals that thought is experienced as an adventure, 'a risk' in Socrates' words, a stretching of the whole person to extend the barriers of spiritual perception. And as the thought cannot be divorced from the thinker, so the philosophy (however abstract) is expressive of the particular disposition of the thinker and the times in which he lives. Thus the concerns of Socrates' dialogues are rooted in the Greek City States at the moment when the inherited mythology was beginning to lose its hold on the consciousness of man. The 'cogito ergo sum' of Descartes comes at the end of the Mediaeval communal world-picture and at the beginning of the Enlightenment. The assertion of Kierkegaard – 'truth is subjectivity' – explodes into the nineteenth century when Faith had become compromised and a fanatical belief in Pure Objectivity become dominant.

At this point I must quickly return to our banal starting point (that education takes place inside the person) for I hope we have reached a stage in the argument where we can both see what important truth lies dormant in the assertion but, also, where it may stand in need of qualification. We have seen that education cannot, meaningfully, take place outside of the assenting individual, but that individual, we have suggested, does not exist outside of the torrent of pressures – pressures of the family, the school, friends, neighbours, history – which constitute his outer world. Indeed from the moment of birth we are let loose on a rushing stream of sensations, and (very soon after that) signs, symbols and artifacts. To exist (*ex-istere*) is to find ourselves beyond ourselves, irredeemably out in a number of worlds that have their own rhythms and patterns and that are yet wound into one multitudinous experience, the experience of each existing individual. It is in individual experience – and only there – that I and the many interacting worlds of Nature, Time, Relationships, History, come together in an intricate, creative, and largely unconscious manifold.

Our obvious proposition no longer seems so certain or so accurate. Rather than to repair it with a qualification, it may be better to cast anew, for in the category of experience, which is neither the objective universe nor the subjective self but the wedding of the two ('my world', 'your world') we arrive at the foundation we are seeking for the discipline of autobiography. It is instructive to note here the etymological root of the word 'experience'. *Experience* comes from the Latin word *experientia*, denoting *the act of trying*. The root-meaning points us to one important truth about experience: it is *not*, as Locke and the empirical tradition would have us accept, passive. It is not made

up by sense-impressions passively recorded on the retina of the
eye and inscribed on the *tabula rasa* of the mind, for –

> This, as Blake insists with all the force of the creative imagina-
> tion, is to deny the essential creativeness of life, and to be
> committed, therefore, to repressing life itself. Perception, he
> insists, in art and aphorism, is creative, and there is a con-
> tinuity from the creativeness of perception to the creativeness
> of the artist.

(F. R. Leavis: *English – Unrest and Continuity*)

Experience, as is suggested by its etymological origin, is assertive,
creative, intentional. Although we are thrown out into the world
in which we move and have our being, we yet create and recreate
in our experience our vision of this world. As Vico said, with
aphoristic concentration, 'We can know nothing that we have
not made'.

Education, then, building on these foundations, is that power
within experience which seeks to develop, refine, increase and
deepen those truths created by experience: and here, one has to
quickly add, the experience of *this* person here, *that* person there.
As a corollary to this, it follows that the enemies of education are
to be associated with those powers which, for whatever reason –
commercial, political, social – blunt, desiccate, corrupt or destroy
the positive urges, the hidden longings infolded in each man's
response to the world. Paradoxically education, in its institu-
tionalized form, can be the enemy of education in its true form.

What I hope I have shown is that education is not primarily
concerned with the accumulation of facts and techniques but
rather with the expression and clarification of individual experience. The centre of education resides in the individual. If we are
to achieve a genuinely human education we must return again
and again to the person before us, the child, the adolescent, the
adult, the individual who is ready, however dimly and in need
of however much support, to adventure both further out into his
experience and further into it, who is ready, in some part of
himself, to risk himself in order to become more than he now is.
The teacher, the tutor, can provide the conditions and the
support for such a journey – but the journey itself can only be
made by the assenting and autonomous individual.

We are now in a position to see the important value of the
discipline of autobiography in the training of teachers and to
counter the arguments of those who would dismiss such a course

as an indulgence or a mere trimming to decorate the hard centre of the conventional syllabus. If the reader agrees that the source of education must reside in the experience of the individual, then a preoccupation with facts and techniques in our Colleges and Departments of Education not only misses the target but aims in the wrong direction. A richer and more fitting approach would seek, through creative understanding, to reveal the intimate relationship between being and knowing, between existence and education, between self and culture. Here we stand at the steps leading to the act of autobiography – for how better to explore the infinite web of connections which draws self and world together in one evolving *gestalt* than through the act of autobiography in which the student will recreate his past and trace the growth of his experience through lived time and felt relationships? What better way to assert the nature of true knowledge than to set the student ploughing the field of his own experience? In hunting out those truths that were so close to him he did not notice them, may he not discover that 'education' is a dusty and much-abused word to denote that action of the inward spirit, by which, often with difficulty, one discovers who one is?

In his *Journals* Kierkegaard described the order of knowledge I have been defending in this introduction as follows:

> It is the divine side of man, his inward action which means everything, not a mass of information; for that will certainly follow and then all that knowledge will not be a chance assemblage, or a succession of details, without system and without a focussing point.

True knowledge is existential knowledge. The act of autobiography, above all, reveals to the student the truth of this proposition, and, in so doing, prepares him to become a responsible and responsive teacher. Who is better equipped to bring education alive than one who knows through his inmost experience what education is? Having outlined briefly the educational and philosophical basis for a course in autobiography, I would like now to consider more closely the nature of the discipline it entails.

2. The Nature of Autobiography

The central concern of all autobiography is to describe, evoke and generally recreate the development of the author's experience.

It is probably in all cases an attempt to answer the following conscious or half-conscious questions: Who am I? How have I become who I am? What may I become in the future? Autobiography is, thus, concerned with time: not the time of the clock, but the time in which we live our lives, with its three tenses of past, present and future. Autobiography, as an act of writing, perches in the present, gazing backwards into the past while poised ready for flight into the future.

The past tense is the most obvious tense of autobiography and needs little elaboration here. Rousseau declares in his *Confessions*: 'To know me in my advanced years you must have known me well in my youth.' The deepest roots of our identity penetrate into the forgotten depths of the past. Even Sartre, who insists in his philosophy on the revolutionary freedom man has to determine his identity, concedes in his autobiography: 'All the characteristics of the child, worn, defaced, humiliated, huddled in a corner and passed over in silence, have survived in the fifty-year-old man.' Indeed, autobiography, the intense recreation of the author's past, reveals a deeper power than freedom in our lives: the power of individuation. Edmund Gosse's *Father and Son* is fascinating in this respect. The extraordinarily powerful pressures of his background (and in particular, of his father) urged him, as a child, to reduce life to a series of objects and facts which could be tabulated, neatly and abstractly: 'The system on which I was being educated deprived all things, human life among the rest, of their mystery. The "bare-grinning skeleton of death" was to me merely a prepared specimen of that featherless, plantigrade vertebrate, "homosapiens".' Yet, again and again, *Father and Son* reveals how the suppressed part of the child's psyche triumphantly asserts itself. Edmund finds 'an indescribable rapture' in the pages of a sensational novel which he discovers by chance lining the inside of a trunk. He has phantasies whereby he believes he can magically bring to life his father's clinical drawings of butterflies and birds. In the garden, mysteriously, he experiences a sudden illumination: 'There was a secret in this world and it belonged to me and to a somebody who lived in the same body with me.' The innate identity, the inward and essential character of the self, will find itself, even when the forces that circumscribe it are hostile and alien. Autobiography is the search backwards into time to discover the evolution of the true self.

At the same time, however, I have described autobiography as being poised for flight into the future. It may have struck the reader as strange to stress the future tense in a form of writing which is so palpably preoccupied with the past. And yet in the conclusions to autobiography one is invariably aware of this submerged concern with the immediate future boldly surfacing. A student, for example, who has courageously grappled with the burden of her own past, finishes her autobiography looking towards the horizons:

> My parents did not know me till that moment, but they do now. They helped me back to my feet, supported me on loving crutches. Perhaps my life would have been so much different if they had known me and I would not be what I am. It's too late to repair but it's early days to understand myself.

Here one senses both a sober acceptance of what has been together with a calm purposeful gazing into the future. Even in the act of remembering, present and future needs play a decisive role. In some students' work one is aware of a hesitancy, perhaps even a reluctance, about remembering past experiences:

> Although one doesn't realise it I suppose to a certain extent the present is dictated by the past . . .
> I suppose my early childhood must have been quite unsettled.
> . . . Perhaps I like to imagine it that way!

The reluctance may be caused by the initial difficulty of remembering in the present, events that lurk dimly on the furthest edges of consciousness or seem, in reason's estimation, to be unutterably trivial. Yet it is true, as Stendhal discovered, that by concentration one can recall more and more of childhood experiences one had thought irretrievably lost. One memory invariably opens a door to another, taking the autobiographer further and further down the passage of time. (When students read excerpts from their work in progress, I have found that quite often one account of a childhood game or event will release in those who are listening a flow of memories till then lost.)

But the hesitant and uncertain tone of some students' autobiography may have another source which I would like briefly to discuss. In *Love and Will*, Rollo May asserts that we only remember those past events and inner feelings which we are capable, at that point in time, of assimilating into our personalities.

> We are . . . unable to give attention to something until we are able in some way to experience an 'I can' with regard to it

> . . . . *Memory is a function of intentionality*. Memory is like perception in this respect; the patient cannot remember something until he is ready to take some stand toward it.

This is a most important observation and sheds particular light on why, in certain students' autobiographies, we detect a nervous evasiveness, an unwillingness to step into dangerous territory, a complex detour around some massively silent obstacle. This must be accepted and respected; it is not the task of the tutor to bludgeon memory where, for its own deep reasons, it is unwilling to go. The terms of each autobiography can only be provided by the individual student: the student should be urged to go only where he feels himself ready to go. But, at the same time, the tutor must be there to provide, should it be necessary, a support —for he, too, having made a similar journey into the self must know the difficulties that may lie in wait.

The autobiographer's memory, to adapt Rollo May's formulation, will be in the service of his own deeper intentionality. This means, in effect, that the student will be happy to recreate those memories which he is ready to take some stand towards. In practice, it means that a number of students, with their interest in educational ideals, will elect to confine their autobiographies to their schooling. This, as well as providing a safely defined area for exploration into the nature of the evolving self, constitutes an excellent preparation for teaching experience. The gifted teacher is always able in his imagination to see the classroom with the child's eye. The writing of autobiography nurtures this power. In their writing, the students rediscover the child's evaluation of his teachers. Consider, for example, the following shrewd assessment of a teacher recalled in one student's autobiography:

> Mr Taylor, harsh man, fond of the slipper and loud voice, kept me subdued. I like writing but get carried away so that often I missed words (or letters) out in my eagerness. He was brutal to me over this—he liked to twist my hair where it was short around my ears and point accusingly at the offending omission while I writhed and apologised. At an open day for parents he smiled ingratiatingly and told Mum that 'Peter's only fault is his brain is quicker than his pencil but that's nothing to worry about'. I loathed him for his deceit.

Or consider the assumption a small child may have about the underlying nature of the teacher as described in another autobiography:

I first articulated my opinion of teachers when I was about 6 or 7. Somehow I got into conversation with one of our teachers who was always very pleasant to me.
—Why are you a teacher? I asked.
—Oh, well, because I like children, she said, rather surprised.
—But I thought teachers had to hate children.
—Oh, no, you have to like children if you're to be a teacher.
I was taken aback by the apparent illogicality of this remark.

Or the way in which a teacher's response may change a child's innocent actions into not so innocent strategies:

As long as I owned up and apologised to the persons involved there was no need for me to worry and I think this was the correct way to treat such cases. However, there was one teacher called Mr Wickham (who very quickly became 'Wickham Wackham') who treated my jangling physical co-ordination with some degree of wrath. He automatically assumed that to break something was a conscious and deliberate act. Such a person seems to push one from genuine clumsiness into calculated error.

Great advances in understanding and sympathy can be gained by the collaborative consideration of the student's experiences of schooling. From a strongly-felt personal basis discussion can profitably develop about the nature and practice of education, both as it was and as it might have been.

Yet, for many, such public discourse will only be *one* level of involvement, pertinent and valuable yet not the deepest. A considerable number of students will welcome the discipline of autobiography in the manner of an inward quest. These students are ready to remember, to recall and to integrate into their identity the whole confused substance of the past. They welcome this opportunity to escape, for a time, the endless demands, distractions, commitments of the outer world. They intuitively know that 'nothing can be sole or whole that has not been rent', and realize the truth recorded in A.E.'s poem:

> In ancient shadows and twilights
> Where childhood had strayed,
> The world's great sorrows were born
> And its heroes were made.
> In the lost childhood of Judas
> Christ was betrayed.

These students know on impulse that education, in its richest form, embraces the whole enigmatic force of life and, in their own writing, work to gain hold of it. This is no simple matter:

> I don't expect this to be easy. I shall need to add to it con-
> tinuously and hope that it represents something reasonable by
> the time it is finished. The beginning must be the most difficult
> of all to write – groping in the dark – later, when other people
> have talked and I have something to compare myself with, I
> might be able to rationalise.

The metaphor 'groping in the dark' conveys well the uncertain probing that characterizes the more ambitious autobiography – the autobiography which is prepared to embrace or soberly acknowledge truths that, before the act of writing, seemed pressing yet murky and elusive. As the following passages show this is not 'easy' and may take the writer, where he is ready for such a confrontation, back to traumatic childhood experiences and early and late adolescent experiences:

> The child walked towards the door and turned the handle,
> quickly pushed open the door and shut it behind her. Looking
> neither to left nor right she marched sturdily towards the door
> that led to the stairs. She opened the door but as she turned to
> close it behind her, in the shaft of light from the hall she saw it,
> a long narrow wooden box. She opened the other door and
> dashed quickly up the stairs to her bedroom. Once there she
> threw herself upon the bed, body heaving with emotion.
> She got up and went to make a cup of coffee. Yes, that was
> the time when everything changed, the time when her brother
> died and she started turning into herself, a reserve which she
> realised now would always be an intrinsic part of herself.

> I was lying in bed one night with my arms outside the blankets
> – they suddenly turned into chicken's legs, bony, scrawny – *old*.
> Everyone seemed in a hurry to grow up at grammar school, I
> just wanted to go on being a child. I remember when I was
> about 11 being panicky about having to stop playing with
> dolls. I knew people would laugh at me if they found out but
> I couldn't bear the thought of giving up for ever my little
> phantasy world in which my dolls were so important. I remem-
> ber walking to school with a group of friends – I was about 14

– one of them was talking about Christmas, she wanted clothes, records, a record player. I said all I wanted was a new hutch for my rabbit, and they all laughed.

'Yes Dad, I'll let you know how I get on.' But I could not help but feel that the gulf between our lives was widening. How could I stop it? Was this not the process of growing up, should I turn away from the future before me, and return to a house and some people I had always known? Unconsciously we had reached that final cross-roads where our paths diverged. Out of touch, out of sight, we had taken each other for granted and it was too late for a re-evaluation of our personal relations.

In such writing the mind does not shy away from anything. As in tragedy 'it does not protect itself with any illusion, it stands uncomforted, unintimidated, alone and self-reliant'.[1] And, curiously, it is often followed with a feeling of liberation – even joy:

I find, in spite of never having talked to this intensity in a group situation that I can follow people's flow, trains of thought. Am delighted, in Leeds I was thick academically. And I had always to feel inferior, quite irrationally. Now I go away exhilarated even if it has seemed an unresponsive afternoon. I am always reworking, always thinking, none of it is ever futile.

Such are the creative moments, pressing into the future which autobiography, as I have argued in this section, is poised ready to fly into. Here, indeed, the way back is the way forward, and the reward, if it can be reached, an enhanced affirmation of the self. For a few students not only plough the field of their experience: they are also able to seed it for a harvest that may be theirs tomorrow. This, I would argue, is the deepest achievement made possible for the student of education through the discipline of autobiography.

3. The Origins of Autobiography

The discipline of autobiography which I am advocating is primarily an inward and creative discipline centred on the

[1] I. A. Richards's description of tragedy in *Principles of Literary Criticism*.

related acts of reflecting on and re-creating the personal past. It is not academic. It begins and ends with what is given in experience. And yet it is of more than casual interest to see how the autobiographical form of writing has developed – for here, too, in our cultural past we discover the roots of our identity penetrating further back than we had imagined. In confronting St Augustine's *Confession* we find ourselves at unexpected points, gazing at our own reflection. We encounter in St Augustine's autobiography that trembling and sustained inwardness which is one of the marks of Western Man and which derives from the powerful influence of the Hebraic religion on his being.

But why, we need to ask, hadn't the form of autobiography emerged before St Augustine? Why hadn't the Greeks, who had developed and perfected so many symbolic forms, created auto-biography? Matthew Arnold in *Culture and Anarchy* provides us with a clue to the answer when he describes the characteristic disposition of Hellenic man:

> To get rid of one's ignorance, to see things as they are, and by seeing them as they are to see them in their beauty, is the simple and attractive ideal which Hellenism holds out before human nature – and from the simplicity and charm of this idea, Hellenism, is invested with a kind of aerial ease, clearness and radiancy: they are full of what we call sweetness and light. Difficulties are kept out of view, and the beauty and rational-ness of the ideal have all our thoughts.

It was just such an informing belief in lucid reason which urged the Greeks to look for fixed and permanent truths, eternal essences, outside of the inward flux of man's own mixed and contrary experience. So absolute was the belief in reason that for Aristotle it came to define man's essential nature. In his *Ethics* he observed: 'What is naturally proper to every creature is the highest and pleasantest for him. And so, to man, this will be the life of Reason, since Reason is, in the highest sense, a man's self.' It is true that the power of reason is one of the defining char-acteristics of man's nature, yet, at the same time, reason follows the line which leads from the specific to the abstract, from the existential to the essential. Reason transports the individual out of his own life and time and surroundings and houses him in logical necessities and radiant ideals. For Plato, ideas were luminous and eternal while existence was dark and mortal. Given such a dominant assumption, it is not surprising that no true form of autobiography emerged in Greek culture, for what the autobiographer relishes – the intimate texture, the fleeting impression, the flash of light at the end of a dim corridor, the fragrant smell which haunts the mind; in fact, all those memories which take the writer spiralling inwards – is what the Greek mind would have dismissed as second-order reality, ephemeral illusions, insignificant shadows unworthy of the attention of a great writer or thinker. Because the deep and problematic nature of experience was not considered a primary reality, any great act of autobiography, in which the writer plunges into his own multitudinous and unique existence, was rendered impossible. In his book *Design and Truth in Autobiography*, Roy Pascal states the case quite simply by declaring that in Greek and Roman civilization 'never was the unique personal story in its private as well as public aspect considered worthy of single-minded devotion of the author'.

It was thus left to St Augustine, at the time of the dissolution of the Roman Empire, to write the first deep autobiography. Again in his book, Roy Pascal pinpoints the essential quality that made the Confessions spiritually and artistically different from any writing which had preceded it.

> Out of memory he [St Augustine] re-collects the scattered pieces of his personality, not in order to demonstrate himself as an Aristotelian entelechy, perfected from the beginning: not like Marcus Aurelius to construct a basic model: but to show his spiritual evolution, the coming-into-being of his full personality – a process of such startling change that he must ascribe it to Divine intervention. . . .
>
> Deeds are not recounted because they occurred, but because they represent stages of spiritual growth.

In the phrase 'spiritual evolution' Roy Pascal defines the essential quality of the *Confessions*. The notion of evolution, of rational development, would not have been alien to Greek civilization – but the notion of spiritual evolution, with the connotations of febrile inwardness that Augustine gives to it, certainly would have. The special dimension, which Augustine's introspective intellect habitually inhabits, comes not from the Greek but from Hebraic culture. Here in the conflict between two cultures we discover, I believe, one of the reasons why Augustine was the first man to write a true autobiography.

In St Augustine the Hebraic stream of Faith and the Hellenic stream of Reason met and the confluence was as productive as it was turbulent. When such great contraries are drawn together, psychic tension is engendered which if it does not destroy the individual mind (for ideas only live in individual minds) is creative of new vision. In St Augustine's *Confessions*, though not in his theology which develops within the Greek framework, man is hurled by his dark and passionate nature beyond the order of knowledge and the control of the will. The ancient unity of the Greeks, depending on the all-embracing energy of the intellect, is irreparably broken, for in Augustine *we are always more than we can know*. 'There is,' declares St Augustine, 'in man an area which not even the *spirit of man* knows of'. And again: 'There is in me a lamentable darkness in which my latent possibilities are hidden from myself, so that my mind, questioning itself upon its own powers, feels it cannot rightly trust its own report.' In confronting such a limitation to knowledge, the essential questions of philosophy became introspective and existential. The question asked by the Greeks '*What* is man?' was transformed into the more pressing question '*Who* is man?' And with the asking of the question, new acts of human attention were made possible, new areas of consciousness discovered. One of these acts of attention was autobiography which allowed a writer to explore nakedly and without apology the unchartered territory of himself. The *Confessions* are, as Peter Brown rightly says in his biography of Augustine, 'a manifesto of the inner world', a turning away from the mechanical and public to the beauties and dangers of the inward soul.

The question 'Who am I?' which draws existentialist philosophy and autobiography together, also had, I suspect, another source. The radical question erupted in the mind of the responsive individual at that point in history when the continuation of man was felt to be uncertain. The *Confessions* were written at the end of the seventh century when the Roman Empire was in a state of rapid and seemingly irresistible dissolution. We discover in Augustine's writing the image of a society which has degenerated into a besotted mob craving for ever more violent and bloody spectacles. Augustine's comments on his friend Alipius who was, before his conversion, pulled into the whirlpool of corrupt fashion, burn into the reader and, at the same time, portray the vicious undercurrents let loose by a civilization in decline:

For as soon as he beheld that blood (the blood of Christians in the amphitheatre) he drank down with it a kind of savageness; he did not now turn away but fastened his gaze upon it, and drinking up the cup of fury ere he knew it, he became enamoured with the wickedness of those combats, and drunk with a delight in blood. He was no more the Alipius who had come there, but one of the common herd with which he came, and an entire companion of those that lead him. What shall I say more? He gazed, he shouted, he burned with the desire of it, and he carried home from thence such a measure of madness as provoked him to return, not only with them by whom he was formerly debauched, but more earnestly than they even going so far as to seduce others also.

In those periods when the configuration of inherited meanings, values, aspirations have either become corrupt or devoid of vitality, the responsive individual is compelled, by the power of his personality reacting to the times, to search out a vision of man which transcends the mediocrity or savagery around him. Fifteen centuries after Augustine, Kierkegaard and Nietzche found themselves outside Christendom, for Christianity in the nineteenth century had become complacent, hypocritical and lost in the daily pressures of what Blake called 'single vision'. It was their turn to face Christianity, the religion which St Augustine had so passionately embraced and disseminated, with the same radical question (Who is man?) and the same inward desire for spiritual transformation. It is also pertinent here to quote from the introduction to Herbert Read's gentle autobiography written in the middle of our own century:

The death wish that was once an intellectual fiction has now become a hideous reality and mankind drifts indifferently to self-destruction. To arrest that drift is beyond our individual capacities, to establish one's individuality is perhaps the only possible protest.

The impulse to write derives from the desire to enrich one's identity *against* the destructiveness of the age. A negative age drives the creator inwards. In Van Gogh's intensely disturbing and unflinchingly honest self-portraits one discovers again, the truth of this assertion. 'The madness of the circus', to use Augustine's words, drives the individual into himself to forge an inner sequence of meanings where the outer ones have collapsed. Against the brutal and the banal, the creator goes in quest of those transcendent energies without which no human life can survive long.

Nietzsche declared in *Thus Spake Zarathustra*: 'One must have chaos within one to give birth to a dancing star.' His illuminating epigram takes us one step further into answering our question: why did autobiography begin in the fourth century in Western Civilization? There was, as we have seen, in St Augustine's time, chaos without: but in the *Confessions* one senses more than this: one is made powerfully aware of chaos exploding within. It is in St Augustine's own personality, in his guilts, in his forebodings, in his lusts, aspirations, anxieties, hopes that one detects that chaos which, perhaps most of all, helped to give birth to the dancing star of autobiography. St Augustine's trembling emotions cannot, it is true, be divorced from the two forces we have already delineated: the confluence of Reason and Faith: the turmoil of the period: and yet the reader of the *Confessions* senses a stormy energy beyond these which can only be located at the centre of Augustine's own personality.

William James in his classic study *The Varieties of Religious Experience* defines brilliantly the temperament of St Augustine. It will be remembered that William James distinguished between the temperament of the 'first born' and that of the 'twice-born'. The former, he writes:

> . . . are born with an inner constitution which is harmonious and well-balanced from the outset. Their impulses are consistent with one another, their will follows without trouble the guidance of their intellect, their passions are not excessive, and their lives are little haunted by regrets.

Whereas the 'twice-born' are persons

> whose existence is little more than a series of zig-zags, as now one tendency and now another gets the upper hand. Their spirit wars with their flesh, they wish for incompatibles, wayward impulses interrupt their most deliberate plans, and their lives are one long drama of repentance and effort to repair misdemeanours and mistakes.

Later on in the same chapter entitled significantly *The Divided Self* William James adds to this description declaring that: 'The man's interior is a battle-ground for what he feels to be two deadly hostile selves, one actual, the other ideal'. There can be no doubt that Augustine, in every respect, belongs with the twice-born. His life, as revealed in his autobiography, is out of harmony: a constant prey to haunting motions, irrational impulses, deep transcendental longings. Again and again the *Confessions* sketch a world that is elusive, enigmatic and paradoxical:

> And if any prosperity smiled upon me, it grieved me to appre-
> hend it, because, almost before I could close my hand upon it,
> it fled away.
> I became unto myself an enigma, and I would ask my soul
> why it was sad, and why it inflicted me so vehemently, yet it
> could make no answer.
> While I thus desired a happy life, I yet feared to seek it in its
> true abode, and I fled from it while yet I sought it.

These lyrical formulations of inner discord characterize the *Confessions* and reveal why it was that St Augustine, in an age in which the daily surface of life was splintering into a thousand parts, was the first man driven to write the history of his own identity.

The lucidity of rational knowledge had provided an escape-route from those truths, those visions, those dreams, those fathom-less desires stirring strangely within. With St Augustine, through the instrument of autobiography, man once again sought to return to those primary sources of Being which the excessive cultivation of Reason and the turning of the community into a mob-collectivity had done so much to obscure.

St Augustine is commonly known as one of the founding fathers of the Christian Church: but for us, as teachers and writers, he should, perhaps, be better known as the father of Autobiography and Existentialism.

In St Augustine's *Confessions* the two main concerns of my introduction, the act of autobiography, the nature of existential truth, come together. William Barret's analysis of St Augustine in his book *Irrational Man* crystallizes the central argument I am making and I would, therefore, like to quote from it at length:

> The existentialism of St Augustine lies in his power as a religious
> psychologist, as expressed most notably and dramatically in his
> *Confessions*. Augustine had almost a voluptuous sensitivity to the
> Self in its inner inquietude, its trembling and frailty, its longing
> to reach beyond itself in love; and in the *Confessions* he gives us a
> revelation of subjective experience such as even the greatest

Hellenic literature does not, and could not, because this interiorisation of experience came through Christianity and was unknown to the earlier Greeks. Where Plato and Aristotle had asked the question What is man? St Augustine (in the *Confessions*) asks Who am I? – and the shift is decisive. The first question presupposed a world of objects, a fixed natural and zoological order, in which man was included. . . . Augustine's question . . . implies that man cannot be defined by being located in that natural order, for man, as the being who asks himself Who am I? has already broken through the barriers of the animal world. Augustine thus opens the door to an altogether different view of man than had prevailed in Greek thought.

Thirteen and a half centuries were to pass before the next great autobiography was to triumphantly (and somewhat indulgently) enter the same door to explore the labyrinthine caverns of the self. Rousseau's *Confessions* written in 1765 and published in 1781 proclaimed in another Age of Reason the formative powers of the emotions in the regulating of human life. Rousseau's long and passionate book was to usher in the age of autobiography. In the following decades many of the major writers: Goethe, Wordsworth, Coleridge, Mill, Gosse, Ruskin, Trollope, Tolstoy, Gorki, were to turn back to their childhood for sustenance, understanding and inspiration.

4. Tutor and Students

The most demanding work for the student engaged in the discipline of autobiography will remain the individual attempt to grapple with his past experience. Many will find this difficult. They will find themselves, perhaps for the first time in their education, facing a series of problems (about what to include, what to exclude, how to begin) which are inherently personal. The tutor can suggest possibilities but he cannot, and should not seek to, solve the student's dilemmas. And the student must remain at all times free to reject the proffered suggestions.

The tutor's main task, I would argue, is often to clarify what is dimly implicit in the student's experience through a series of questions. At the beginning of one tutorial in which the students were gathering to read for the first time excerpts from their first drafts, one mature student looked up and said:

'Does it have to be personal?'

'How do you mean?' I asked.

'I mean written in the first person,' she said.

'Gorki's autobiography was written in the third person,' I answered. That was enough. The student took out her writing pad and scrawled for a few minutes. Then she read out what she had written:

> Her earliest memories consisted of short, brief, bright pictures: tea bushes, coolies, brilliant flowers, heat, all merging into a canvas of flat colour. The first concrete memory, incorporating picture, sound and emotion did not come until about three and a half years old. That memory did not need extracting from a whole, it was complete in itself. White – white shorts, white shirt, white socks. She'd demanded that he wear white, as she remembered him, but had forgotten how huge he was. Still, the thought of the surprise they had brought overcame her awe and, grabbing his hand, she dragged him to the cabin. Pointing to a cot on the bunk she said, 'Daddy, look what we've brought you'.
>
> Again and again she probed back, trying to piece the fragments of colour, people, places and warmth into a comprehensible pattern. They merged for a moment, only to be lost again in a shifting mist. Again she reached out and grasped a memory and lost it. What emerged finally, perhaps covered a space of four years, but time itself was irrelevant, as the events could have been separated by minutes, hours or months.

The student had suddenly found that she could best capture her childhood by employing a third-person narrative. For some reason, an impersonal method of writing released her imagination and freed her memory which until then had been constricted by the direct first-person presentation we normally associate with autobiography. Another student, without prior discussion, intuitively used the third person to convey (and also to distance) the more harrowing experiences of his past and used the first-person narrative to evoke the more leisurely and happy moments. In every case, the form chosen, the style used, is expressive of the person writing and constitutes an essential part of the autobiography. The tutor may provoke, question, compare and contrast, but, in the end, the student, the autobiographer, must decide *how* he will write and *what* must be his proper subject-matter.

Where, then, does the study of the tradition of autobiography – the study, for example, of St Augustine, Rousseau, Mill and Gorki – come in? I think there are two ways in which the tutor can draw on this material.

First of all he can regard it as a secondary source of autobiographical material which he can introduce, where needed, to deepen or amplify or interpret the turmoil of experience thrown up in his students' work. Let me give one example. A student expressing a moment of illumination in her childhood, wrote:

About halfway along the road to adulthood I went through a very strange experience. A psychiatrist could probably explain it away in a few well chosen words. It baffled me. At seven I had the sudden and world shattering realisation that I was a human being, an individual, responsible to and for myself. Only I could think my thoughts, I was not a part of the adults around me. This revelation was at once exciting and terrifying. What would happen to me if my mother died? Should I have to go into a home? How does one arrange a funeral?

Such an experience could gain by being sympathetically compared to those experiences of 'being I' that Gosse records in his *Father and Son* or to Jung's description in his autobiography *Memories, Dreams, Reflections* of becoming self-conscious at a very early age:

I was taking the long road from school from Klein-Huningen, where we lived to Basel, when suddenly for a single moment I had the overwhelming impression of having just emerged from a dense cloud. I knew all at once: now *I am myself*! It was as if a wall of mist were at my back, and behind that wall there was not yet an 'I'. But at this moment *I came upon* myself. Previously I had existed too, but everything had merely happened to me. Now I happened to myself. Now I knew: I am myself now, now I exist. Previously I had been willed to do this and that: now I willed. This experience seemed to me tremendously important and new: there was 'authority' in me.

To introduce Gosse's and Jung's autobiography at this particular point would be to confirm the student's own uncanny realization of self and, in the context of the seminar, to make such an experience a more accessible part of our human reality.

Secondly, the great autobiographies can be considered on their own terms. The tutor, if he wishes to embark on such a study, can best decide when the students will gain most from it. Clearly some autobiography could be introduced in this manner as a means of beginning the whole project. Here Gorki's *My Childhood* and Herbert Read's *The Contrary Experience* being so direct and so lyrically powerful provide excellent starting points. A more detailed consideration of autobiography – including a discussion of the philosophical issues I raised earlier – is probably best reserved until after the student's own work is completed.

I would like, finally, to clarify a number of points.

In the discussion-periods which I suggested earlier should take place once a week and last a minimum of one hour, I invited each student to read an excerpt from his own autobiography which, at that point, was in process of being written. Some students read only a few excerpts from their work. Others chose to read, week by week, their whole script.[1] Here the tutor's influence must be subtle and indirect. Any compulsion is alien to the liberating spirit of autobiography. By his presence the tutor must be able to create the feel of trust: that trust in which each student feels able to present himself, to be who he is. If this spirit of trust and collaboration can be established, the weekly meeting becomes an essential focus to the work. The meeting provides the private act of autobiography with a valuable public face. The student knows he is not plunging into his identity alone. He is doing it with others, and often, at the meetings, he is gaining as much from their descent as his own. The mutuality engendered need not be explicit. It is most powerful and real where it is tacit and assumed: for as one student pointed out –

> There is a certain amount of honesty among us that might be lost if we analyse our reactions too much.

I think an invisible strength is given to the work if the students know that the tutor also, has attempted to embrace parts of his own childhood. Again this need never be more explicit than the tutor saying or implying 'I know what it is like'. I have for this reason included in this book my own sketch in autobiography. It is not there for comparison. It is there to personally demonstrate

[1] It may also be worth pointing out that the student's autobiography need not be handed in in its entirety. If there are certain experiences which, for personal or professional reasons, the student does not wish the tutor to know about, then there is no reason why the tutor should read those chapters which describe them. This freedom protects both student and tutor.

my conviction that we cannot ask others to risk themselves in the name of education, unless we have done so or are willing to ourselves.

In writing 'My Vocation' I discovered, with a certain alarm, that imagination will change outward events in order to articulate an essential truth. Such a remark, I realize, raises a new host of questions about the nature of autobiography. This is not the place to ask them or to answer them. It must suffice for me to state that my own limited attempt encouraged me to see numerous ways of approaching autobiography (many of them subsequently to be given form by my students) and to realize, on my pulse, that autobiographical truth is, in essence, inner truth, immeasurable and, if we so will it, inviolable.

II From Writers' Autobiographies

1. St Augustine: *Confessions*

St Augustine (354–430) was born into a small land-owning family in Thagaste, North Africa. As a young man he came under the influence of the Manichee movement which believed that matter was evil and spirit good (and hence denied the Virgin Birth and the Crucifixion). He studied at Carthage and in 384 became Professor of Rhetoric in Milan. Later he became Bishop of Hippo in Northern Africa.

Augustine began writing his *Confessions* about 377, eleven years after his conversion to Christianity and a few years after becoming a bishop. His autobiography is, in essence, a great act of therapy which openly looks back at the vicissitudes and failings of his past in order to confess and so transcend them. The work, consisting of thirteen books, is written in the form of a prayer directly addressed to God.

My soul is like a house, small for you to enter, but I pray you to enlarge it. It is in ruins, but I ask you to remake it. It contains much that you will not be pleased to see: this I know and do not hide. But who is to rid it of these things? There is no one but you to whom I can say: *if I have sinned unwittingly, do you absolve me. Keep me ever your own servant, far from pride.*[1] *I trust, and trusting I find words to utter.*[2] Lord, you know that this is true. For have I not *made my transgression known to you?* Did you not *remit the guilt of my sin?*[3] I do not wrangle with you for judgement,[4] for you are Truth itself, and I have no wish to delude myself, for fear that my malice should be self-betrayed.[5] No, I do not wrangle with you, for, *if you, Lord, will keep record of our iniquities, Master, who has strength to bear it?*[6]

But, dust and ashes though I am, let me appeal to your pity, since

---

[1] Ps. 18: 13, 14 (19: 12, 13).   [2] Ps. 115: 10 (116: 10).
[3] Ps. 31: 5 (32: 5).   [4] See Jer. 2: 29.   [5] See Ps. 26: 12 (27: 12).
[6] Ps. 129: 3 (130: 3).

it is to you in your mercy that I speak, not to a man who would simply laugh at me. Perhaps you too may laugh at me, but you will relent and have pity on me.[1] For all I want to tell you, Lord, is that I do not know where I came from when I was born into this life which leads to death – or should I say, this death which leads to life? This much is hidden from me. But, although I do not remember it all myself, I know that when I came into the world all the comforts which your mercy provides were there ready for me. This I was told by my parents, the father who begat me and the mother who conceived me, the two from whose bodies you formed me in the limits of time. So it was that I was given the comfort of woman's milk.

But neither my mother nor my nurses filled their breasts of their own accord, for it was you who used them, as your law prescribes, to give me infant's food and a share of the riches which you distribute even among the very humblest of all created things. It was also by your gift that I did not wish for more than you gave, and that my nurses gladly passed on to me what you gave to them. They did this because they loved me in the way that you had ordained, and their love made them anxious to give to me what they had received in plenty from you. For it was to their own good that what was good for me should come to me from them; though, of course, it did not come to me from them but, through them, from you, because you, my God, are the source of all good and *everywhere you preserve me.*[2] All this I have learned since then, because all the gifts you have given to me, both spiritual and material, proclaim the truth of it. But in those days all I knew was how to suck, and how to lie still when my body sensed comfort or cry when it felt pain.

Later on I began to smile as well, first in my sleep, and then when I was awake. Others told me this about myself, and I believe what they said, because we see other babies do the same. But I cannot remember it myself. Little by little I began to realize where I was and to want to make my wishes known to others, who might satisfy them. But this I could not do, because my wishes were inside me, while other people were outside, and they had no faculty which could penetrate my mind. So I would toss my arms and legs about and make noises, hoping that such few signs as I could make would show my meaning, though they were quite unlike what they were meant to mime. And if my wishes were not

[1] See Jer. 12: 15.
[2] II Kings (2 Sam.) 23: 5.

A.E.—2

carried out, either because they had not been understood or because what I wanted would have harmed me, I would get cross with my elders, who were not at my beck and call, and with people who were not my servants, simply because they did not attend to my wishes; and I would take my revenge by bursting into tears. By watching babies I have learnt that this is how they behave, and they, quite unconsciously, have done more than those who brought me up and knew all about it to convince me that I behaved in just the same way myself.

My infancy is long since dead, yet I am still alive. But you, Lord, live for ever and nothing in you dies, because you have existed from before the very beginning of the ages, before anything that could be said to go before, and you are God and Lord of all you have created. In you are the first causes of all things not eternal, the unchangeable origins of all things that suffer change, the everlasting reason of all things that are subject to the passage of time and have no reason in themselves. Have pity, then, on me, O God, for it is pity that I need. Answer my prayer and tell me whether my infancy followed upon some other stage of life that died before it. Was it the stage of life that I spent in my mother's womb? For I have learnt a little about that too, and I have myself seen women who were pregnant. But what came before that, O God my Delight? Was I anywhere? Was I anybody? These are questions I must put to you, for I have no one else to answer them. Neither my father nor my mother could tell me, nor could I find out from the experience of other people or from my own memory. Do my questions provoke you to smile at me and bid me simply to acknowledge you and praise you for what I do know?

I do acknowledge you, Lord of heaven and earth, and I praise you for my first beginnings, although I cannot remember them. But you have allowed men to discover these things about themselves by watching other babies, and also to learn much from what women have to tell. I know that I was a living person even at that age, and as I came towards the end of infancy I tried to find signs to convey my feelings to others. Where could such a living creature come from if not from you, O Lord? Can it be that any man has skill to fabricate himself? Or can there be some channel by which we derive our life and our very existence from some other source than you? Surely we can only derive them from our Maker, from you, Lord, to whom living and being are not different things, since infinite life and infinite being are one and the same. For you are infinite and never change. In you 'today' never comes to an end: and yet our 'today' does come to an end in you, because time, as well as everything else, exists in you. If it did not, it would have no means of passing. And since your years never come to an end, for you they are simply 'today'. The countless days of our lives and of our forefathers' lives have passed by within your 'today'. From it they have received their due measure of duration and their very existence. And so it will be with all the other days which are still to come. But you yourself are eternally the same. In your 'today' you have made all that existed yesterday and for ever before.

Need it concern me if some people cannot understand this? Let them ask what it means, and be glad to ask: but they may content themselves with the question alone. For it is better for them to find you and leave the question unanswered than to find the answer without finding you.

The next stage in my life, as I grew up, was boyhood. Or would it be truer to say that boyhood overtook me and followed upon my infancy – not that my infancy left me, for, if it did, where did it go? All the same, it was no longer there, because I ceased to be a baby unable to talk, and was now a boy with the power of speech. I can remember that time, and later on I realized how I had learnt to speak. It was not my elders who showed me the words by some set system of instruction, in the way that they taught me to read not long afterwards; but, instead, I taught myself by using the intelligence which you, my God, gave to me. For when I tried to express my meaning by crying out and making various sounds and movements, so that my wishes should be obeyed, I found that I could not convey all that I meant or make myself understood by everyone whom I wished to understand me. So my memory prompted me. I noticed that people would name some object and then turn towards whatever it was that they had named. I watched them and understood that the sound they made when they wanted to indicate that particular thing was the name which they gave to it, and their actions clearly showed what they meant, for there is a kind of universal language, consisting of expressions of the face and eyes, gestures and tones of voice, which can show whether a person means to ask for something and get it, or refuse it and have nothing to do with it. So, by hearing words arranged in various phrases and constantly repeated, I gradually pieced together what they stood for, and when my tongue had mastered the pronunciation, I began to express my wishes by means of them. In this way I made my wants known to my family and they made theirs known to me, and I took a further step into the stormy life of human society, although I was still subject to the authority of my parents and the will of my elders.

But, O God my God, I now went through a period of suffering and humiliation. I was told that it was right and proper for me as a boy to pay attention to my teachers, so that I should do well at my study of grammar and get on in the world. This was the way to gain the respect of others and win for myself what passes for wealth in this world. So I was sent to school to learn to read. I was too small to understand what purpose it might serve and yet, if I was idle at my studies, I was beaten for it, because beating was favoured by tradition. Countless boys long since forgotten had built up this stony path for us to tread and we were made to pass along it, adding to the toil and sorrow of the sons of Adam.

But we found that some men prayed to you, Lord, and we learned from them to do the same, thinking of you in the only way that we could understand, as some great person who could listen to us and help us, even though we could not see you or hear you or touch you. I was still a boy when I first began to pray to you, my Help and Refuge. I used to prattle away to you, and though I was small, my devotion was great when I begged you not to let me be beaten at school. Sometimes, for my own good, you did not grant my prayer, and then my elders and even my parents, who certainly wished me no harm, would laugh at the beating I got – and in those days beatings were my one great bugbear.

O Lord, throughout the world men beseech you to preserve them from the rack and the hook and various similar tortures which terrify them. Some people are merely callous, but if a man clings to you with great devotion, how can his piety inspire him to find it in his heart to make light of these tortures, when he loves those who dread them so fearfully? And yet this was how our parents scoffed at the torments which we boys suffered at the hands of our masters. For we feared the whip just as much as others fear the rack, and we, no less than they, begged you to preserve us from it. But we sinned by reading and writing and studying less than was expected of us. We lacked neither memory nor intelligence, because by your will, O Lord, we had as much of both as was sufficient for our years. But we enjoyed playing games and were punished by men who played games themselves. However, grown-up games are known as 'business', and even though boys' games are much the same, they are punished for them by their elders. No one pities either the boys or the men, though surely we deserved pity, for I cannot believe that a good judge would approve of the beatings I received as a boy on the ground that my games delayed my progress in studying subjects which would enable me to play a less creditable game later in life. Was the master who beat me himself very different from me? If he were worsted by a colleague in some petty argument, he would be convulsed with anger and envy, much more so than I was when a playmate beat me at a game of ball.

It is certain, O Lord, that theft is punished by your law, the law that is written in men's hearts and cannot be erased however sinful they are. For no thief can bear that another thief should steal from him, even if he is rich and the other is driven to it by want. Yet I was willing to steal, and steal I did, although I was not compelled by any lack, unless it were the lack of a sense of justice or a distaste for what was right and a greedy love of doing wrong. For of what I stole I already had plenty, and much better at that, and I had no wish to enjoy the things I coveted by stealing, but only to enjoy the theft itself and the sin. There was a pear-tree near our vineyard, loaded with fruit that was attractive neither to look at nor to taste. Late one night a band of ruffians, myself included, went off to shake down the fruit and carry it away, for we had continued our games out of doors until well after dark, as was our pernicious habit. We took away an enormous quantity of pears, not to eat them ourselves, but simply to throw them to the pigs. Perhaps we ate some of them, but our real pleasure consisted in doing something that was forbidden.

Look into my heart, O God, the same heart on which you took pity when it was in the depths of the abyss. Let my heart now tell you what prompted me to do wrong for no purpose, and why it was only my own love of mischief that made me do it. The evil in me was foul, but I loved it. I loved my own perdition and my own faults, not the things for which I committed wrong, but the wrong itself. My soul was vicious and broke away from your safe keeping to seek its own destruction, looking for no profit in disgrace but only for disgrace itself.

The eye is attracted by beautiful objects, by gold and silver and all such things. There is great pleasure, too, in feeling something agreeable to touch, and material things have various qualities to please each of the other senses. Again, it is gratifying to be held in esteem by other men and to have the power of giving them orders and gaining the mastery over them. This is also the reason why revenge is sweet. But our ambition to obtain all these things must not lead us astray from you, O Lord, nor must we depart from what your law allows. The life we live on earth has its own attractions as well, because it has a certain beauty of its own in harmony with all the rest of this world's beauty. Friendship among men, too, is a delightful bond, uniting many souls in one. All these things and their like can be occasions of sin because, good though they are, they are of the lowest order of good, and if we are too much tempted by them we abandon those higher and better things, your truth, your law, and you yourself, O Lord our God. For these earthly things, too, can give joy, though not such joy as my God, who made them all, can give, because *honest men will rejoice in the Lord; upright hearts will not boast in vain.*[1]

When there is an inquiry to discover why a crime has been committed, normally no one is satisfied until it has been shown that the motive might have been either the desire of gaining, or the fear of losing, one of those good things which I said were of the lowest order. For such things are attractive and have beauty, although they are paltry trifles in comparison with the worth of God's blessed treasures. A man commits murder and we ask the reason. He did it because he wanted his victim's wife or estates for himself, or so that he might live on the proceeds of robbery, or because he was afraid that the other might defraud him of something, or because he had been wronged and was burning for revenge. Surely no one would believe that he would commit murder for no reason but the sheer delight of killing? Sallust tells us that Catiline was a man of insane ferocity, 'who chose to be cruel and vicious without apparent reason';[2] but we are also told that his purpose was 'not to allow his men to lose heart or waste their skill through lack of practice'.[3] If we ask the reason for this, it is obvious that he meant that once he had made himself master of the government by means of this continual violence, he would obtain honour, power, and wealth and would no longer go in fear of the law because of his crimes or have to face difficulties through lack of funds. So even Catiline did not love crime for

---

[1] Ps. 63: 11 (64: 10).   [2] Sallust, *Catilina* xvi.   [3] Sallust, *Catilina* xvi.

crime's sake. He loved something quite different, for the sake of which he committed his crimes.

If the crime of theft which I committed that night as a boy of sixteen were a living thing, I could speak to it and ask what it was that, to my shame, I loved in it. I had no beauty because it was a robbery. It is true that the pears which we stole had beauty, because they were created by you, the good God, who are the most beautiful of all beings and the Creator of all things, the supreme Good and my own true Good. But it was not the pears that my unhappy soul desired. I had plenty of my own, better than those, and I only picked them so that I might steal. For no sooner had I picked them than I threw them away, and tasted nothing in them but my own sin, which I relished and enjoyed. If any part of one of those pears passed my lips, it was the sin that gave it flavour.

And now, O Lord my God, now that I ask what pleasure I had in that theft, I find that it had no beauty to attract me. I do not mean beauty of the sort that justice and prudence possess, nor the beauty that is in man's mind and in his memory and in the life that animates him, nor the beauty of the stars in their allotted places or of the earth and sea, teeming with new life born to replace the old as it passes away. It did not even have the shadowy, deceptive beauty which makes vice attractive – pride, for instance, which is a pretence of superiority, imitating yours, for you alone are God, supreme over all; or ambition, which is only a craving for honour and glory, when you alone are to be honoured before all and you alone are glorious for ever. Cruelty is the weapon of the powerful, used to make others fear them: yet no one is to be feared but God alone, from whose power nothing can be snatched away or stolen by any man at any time or place or by any means. The lustful use caresses to win the love they crave for, yet no caress is sweeter than your charity and no love is more rewarding than the love of your truth, which shines in beauty above all else. Inquisitiveness has all the appearance of a thirst for knowledge, yet you have supreme knowledge of all things. Ignorance, too, and stupidity choose to go under the mask of simplicity and innocence, because you are simplicity itself and no innocence is greater than yours. You are innocent even of the harm which overtakes the wicked, for it is the result of their own actions. Sloth poses as the love of peace: yet what certain peace is there besides the Lord? Extravagance masquerades as fullness and abundance:

but you are the full, unfailing store of never-dying sweetness. The spendthrift makes a pretence of liberality: but you are the most generous dispenser of all good. The covetous want many possessions for themselves: you possess all. The envious struggle for preferment: but what is to be preferred before you? Anger demands revenge: but what vengeance is as just as yours? Fear shrinks from any sudden, unwonted danger which threatens the things that it loves, for its only care is safety: but to you nothing is strange, nothing unforeseen. No one can part you from the things that you love, and safety is assured nowhere but in you. Grief eats away its heart for the loss of things which it took pleasure in desiring, because it wants to be like you, from whom nothing can be taken away.

So the soul defiles itself with unchaste love when it turns away from you and looks elsewhere for things which it cannot find pure and unsullied except by returning to you. All who desert you and set themselves up against you merely copy you in a perverse way; but by this very act of imitation they only show that you are the Creator of all nature and, consequently, that there is no place whatever where man may hide away from you.

What was it, then, that pleased me in that act of theft? Which of my Lord's powers did I imitate in a perverse and wicked way? Since I had no real power to break his law, was it that I enjoyed at least the pretence of doing so, like a prisoner who creates for himself the illusion of liberty by doing something wrong, when he has no fear of punishment, under a feeble hallucination of power? Here was the slave who ran away from his master and chased a shadow instead! What an abomination! What a parody of life! What abysmal death! Could I enjoy doing wrong for no other reason than that it was wrong? *What return shall I make to the Lord*[1] for my ability to recall these things with no fear in my soul? I will love you, Lord, and thank you, and praise your name, because you have forgiven me such great sins and such wicked deeds. I acknowledge that it was by your grace and mercy that you melted away my sins like ice. I acknowledge, too, that by your grace I was preserved from whatever sins I did not commit, for there was no knowing what I might have done, since I loved evil even if it served no purpose. I avow that you have forgiven me all, both the sins which I committed of my own accord and those which by your guidance I was spared from committing.

What man who reflects upon his own weakness can dare to

[1] Ps. 115: 12 (116: 12).

claim that his own efforts have made him chaste and free from sin, as though this entitled him to love you the less, on the ground that he had less need of the mercy by which you forgive the sins of the penitent? There are some who have been called by you and because they have listened to your voice they have avoided the sins which I here record and confess for them to read. But let them not deride me for having been cured by the same Doctor who preserved them from sickness, or at least from such grave sickness as mine. Let them love you just as much, or even more, than I do, for they can see that the same healing hand which rid me of the great fever of my sins protects them from falling sick of the same disease.

It brought me no happiness, for *what harvest did I reap from acts which now make me blush,*[1] particularly from that act of theft? I loved nothing in it except the thieving, though I cannot truly speak of that as a 'thing' that I could love, and I was only the more miserable because of it. And yet, as I recall my feelings at the time, I am quite sure that I would not have done it on my own. Was it then that I also enjoyed the company of those with whom I committed the crime? If this is so, there was something else I loved besides the act of theft; but I cannot call it 'something else', because companionship, like theft, is not a thing at all.

No one can tell me the truth of it except my God, who enlightens my mind and dispels the shadows. What conclusion am I trying to reach from these questions and this discussion? It is true that if the pears which I stole had been to my taste, and if I had wanted to get them for myself, I might have committed the crime on my own if I had needed to do no more than that to win myself the pleasure. I should have had no need to kindle my glowing desire by rubbing shoulders with a gang of accomplices. But as it was not the fruit that gave me pleasure, I must have got it from the crime itself, from the thrill of having partners in sin.

How can I explain my mood? It was certainly a very vile frame of mind and one for which I suffered; but how can I account for it? *Who knows his own frailties?*[2]

We were tickled to laughter by the prank we had played, because no one suspected us of it although the owners were furious. Why was it, then, that I thought it fun not to have been the only culprit? Perhaps it was because we do not easily laugh

[1] Rom. 6: 21.   [2] Ps. 18: 13 (19:12).
A.E.—2*

when we are alone. True enough: but even when a man is all by himself and quite alone, sometimes he cannot help laughing if he thinks or hears or sees something especially funny. All the same, I am quite sure that I would never have done this thing on my own.

My God, I lay all this before you, for it is still alive in my memory. By myself I would not have committed that robbery. It was not the takings that attracted me but the raid itself, and yet to do it by myself would have been no fun and I should not have done it. This was friendship of a most unfriendly sort, bewitching my mind in an inexplicable way. For the sake of a laugh, a little sport, I was glad to do harm and anxious to damage another; and that without thought of profit for myself or retaliation for injuries received! And all because we are ashamed to hold back when others say 'Come on! Let's do it!'

Can anyone unravel this twisted tangle of knots? I shudder to look at it or think of such abomination. I long instead for innocence and justice, graceful and splendid in eyes whose sight is undefiled. My longing fills me and yet it cannot cloy. With them is certain peace and life that cannot be disturbed. The man who enters their domain goes to *share the joy of his Lord*.[1] He shall know no fear and shall lack no good. In him that is goodness itself he shall find his own best way of life. But I deserted you, my God. In my youth I wandered away, too far from your sustaining hand, and created of myself a barren waste.

It was my ambition to be a good speaker, for the unhallowed and inane purpose of gratifying human vanity. The prescribed course of study brought me to a work by an author named Cicero, whose writing nearly everyone admires, if not the spirit of it. The title of the book is *Hortensius* and it recommends the reader to study philosophy. It altered my outlook on life. It changed my prayers to you, O Lord, and provided me with new hopes and aspirations. All my empty dreams suddenly lost their charm and my heart began to throb with a bewildering passion for the wisdom of eternal truth. I began to climb out of the depths to which I had sunk, in order to return to you. For I did not use the book as a whetstone to sharpen my tongue. It was not the style of it but the contents which won me over, and yet the allowance which my mother paid me was supposed to be spent on putting an

[1] Matt. 25:21

edge on my tongue. I was now in my nineteenth year and she supported me, because my father had died two years before.

My God, how I burned with longing to have wings to carry me back to you, away from all earthly things, although I had no idea what you would do with me! For *yours is the wisdom.*[1] In Greek the word 'philosophy' means 'love of wisdom', and it was with this love that the *Hortensius* inflamed me. There are people for whom philosophy is a means of misleading others, for they misuse its great name, its attractions, and its integrity to give colour and gloss to their own errors. Most of these so-called philosophers who lived in Cicero's time and before are noted in the book. He shows them up in their true colours and makes quite clear how wholesome is the admonition which the Holy Spirit gives in the words of your good and true servant, Paul: *Take care not to let anyone cheat you with his philosophizings, with empty fantasies drawn from human tradition, from worldly principles; they were never Christ's teaching. In Christ the whole plenitude of Deity is embodied and dwells in him.*[2]

But, O Light of my heart, you know that at that time, although Paul's words were not known to me, the only thing that pleased me in Cicero's book was his advice not simply to admire one or another of the schools of philosophy, but to love wisdom itself, whatever it might be, and to search for it, pursue it, hold it, and embrace it firmly. These were the words which excited me and set me burning with fire, and the only check to this blaze of enthusiasm was that they made no mention of the name of Christ. For by your mercy, Lord, from the time when my mother fed me at the breast my infant heart had been suckled dutifully on his name, the name of your Son, my Saviour. Deep inside my heart his name remained, and nothing could entirely captivate me, however learned, however neatly expressed, however true it might be, unless his name were in it.

So I made up my mind to examine the holy Scriptures and see what kind of books they were. I discovered something that was at once beyond the understanding of the proud and hidden from the eyes of children. Its gait was humble, but the heights it reached were sublime. It was enfolded in mysteries, and I was not the kind of man to enter into it or bow my head to follow where it led. But these were not the feelings I had when I first read the Scriptures. To me they seemed quite unworthy of comparison with the stately prose of Cicero, because I had too much conceit to

[1] Job 12: 13.   [2] Col. 2: 8, 9.

accept their simplicity and not enough insight to penetrate their depths. It is surely true that as the child grows these books grow with him. But I was too proud to call myself a child. I was inflated with self-esteem, which made me think myself a great man.

I fell in with a set of sensualists, men with glib tongues who ranted and raved and had the snares of the devil in their mouths. They baited the traps by confusing the syllables of the names of God the Father, God the Son Our Lord Jesus Christ, and God the Holy Ghost, the Paraclete, who comforts us. These names were always on the tips of their tongues, but only as sounds which they mouthed aloud, for in their hearts they had no inkling of the truth. Yet 'Truth and truth alone' was the motto which they repeated to me again and again, although the truth was nowhere to be found in them. All that they said was false, both what they said about you, who truly are the Truth, and what they said about this world and its first principles, which were your creation. But I ought not to have been content with what the philosophers said about such things, even when they spoke the truth. I should have passed beyond them for love of you, my supreme Father, my good Father, in whom all beauty has its source.

Truth! Truth! How the very marrow of my soul within me yearned for it as they dinned it in my ears over and over again! To them it was no more than a name to be voiced or a word to be read in their libraries of huge books. But while my hunger was for you, for Truth itself, these were the dishes on which they served me up the sun and the moon, beautiful works of yours but still only your works, not you yourself nor even the greatest of your created things.[1] For your spiritual works are greater than these material things, however brightly they may shine in the sky.

But my hunger and thirst were not even for the greatest of your works, but for you, my God, because you are Truth itself *with whom there can be no change, no swerving from your course*.[2] Yet the dishes they set before me were still loaded with dazzling fantasies, illusions with which the eye deceives the mind. It would have been better to love the sun itself, which at least is real as far as we can see. But I gulped down this food, because I thought that it was you. I had no relish for it, because the taste it left in my mouth was not the taste of truth — it could not be, for it was not you but

[1] St Augustine is here speaking of the Manichees, for whom astronomy was a part of theology.
[2] James 1: 17.

an empty sham. And it did not nourish me, but starved me all the more. The food we dream of is very like the food we eat when we are awake, but it does not nourish because it is only a dream. Yet the things they gave me to eat were not in the least like you, as now I know since you have spoken to me. They were dream-substances, mock realities, far less true than the real things which we see with the sight of our eyes in the sky or on the earth. These things are seen by bird and beast as well as by ourselves, and they are far more certain than any image we conceive of them. And in turn we can picture them to ourselves with greater certainty than the vaster, infinite things which we surmise from them. Such things have no existence at all, but they were the visionary foods on which I was then fed but not sustained.

But you, O God whom I love and on whom I lean in weakness so that I may be strong, you are not the sun and the moon and the stars, even though we see these bodies in the heavens; nor are you those other bodies which we do not see in the sky, for you created them and, in your reckoning, they are not even among the greatest of your works. How far, then, must you really be from those fantasies of mine, those imaginary material things which do not exist at all! The images we form in our mind's eye, when we picture things that really do exist, are far better founded than these inventions; and the things themselves are still more certain than the images we form of them. But you are not these things. Neither are you the soul, which is the life of bodies and, since it gives them life, must be better and more certain than they are themselves. But you are the life of souls, the life of lives. You live, O Life of my soul, because you are life itself, immutable.

Where were you in those days? How far away from me? I was wandering far from you and I was not even allowed to eat the husks on which I fed the swine. For surely the fables of the poets and the penmen are better than the traps which those impostors set! There is certainly more to be gained from verses and poems and tales like the flight of Medea than from their stories of the five elements disguised in various ways because of the five dens of darkness. These things simply do not exist and they are death to those who believe in them. Verses and poems can provide real food for thought, but although I used to recite verses about Medea's flight through the air, I never maintained that they were true; and I never believed the poems which I heard others recite. But I did believe the tales which these men told.

These were the stages of my pitiful fall into the depths of hell, as

I struggled and strained for lack of the truth. My God, you had mercy on me even before I had confessed to you; but I now confess that all this was because I tried to find you, not through the understanding of the mind, by which you meant us to be superior to the beasts, but through the senses of the flesh. Yet you were deeper than my inmost understanding and higher than the topmost height that I could reach. I had blundered upon that woman in Solomon's parable who, ignorant and unabashed, sat at her door and said *Stolen waters are sweetest, and bread is better eating when there is none to see.*[1] She inveigled me because she found me living in the outer world that lay before my eyes, the eyes of the flesh, and dwelling upon the food which they provided for my mind.

2. Jean-Jacques Rousseau: *Confessions*

Rousseau (1712–78) was born in Geneva, the son of a watchmaker. At the age of sixteen, he ran away from the city, breaking his apprenticeship as an engraver, and began a life of wandering. In 1762 he published his revolutionary book on education, *Emile*, and *The Social Contract*. He was heavily persecuted for writing these books and became an exile, first in Geneva, then in England. In the summer of 1770 he was allowed to return to Paris where he spent the last eight years of his life.

Rousseau, opposed to the assumptions of the Enlightenment, believed that feeling, not reason, dictated the course of our actions and when in 1766 he began writing his autobiography (which was not published until after his death) he declared that his life was 'the story of his feelings'. Even at the age of six, he wrote, 'I had no idea of the facts, but I was already familiar with every feeling. I had grasped nothing; I had sensed everything.'

I have resolved on an enterprise which has no precedent, and which, once complete, will have no imitator. My purpose is to display to my kind a portrait in every way true to nature, and the man I shall portray will be myself.

Simply myself. I know my own heart and understand my fellow man. But I am made unlike any one I have ever met; I will even venture to say that I am like no one in the whole world. I may be

[1] Proverbs 9: 17.

no better, but at least I am different. Whether Nature did well or ill in breaking the mould in which she formed me, is a question which can only be resolved after the reading of my book.

Let the last trump sound when it will, I shall come forward with this work in my hand, to present myself before my Sovereign Judge, and proclaim aloud: 'Here is what I have done, and if by chance I have used some immaterial embellishment it has been only to fill a void due to a defect of memory. I may have taken for fact what was no more than probability, but I have never put down as true what I knew to be false, I have displayed myself as I was, as vile and despicable when my behaviour was such, as good, generous, and noble when I was so. I have bared my secret soul as Thou thyself hast seen it, Eternal Being! So let the numberless legion of my fellow men gather round me, and hear my confessions. Let them groan at my depravities, and blush for my misdeeds. But let each one of them reveal his heart at the foot of Thy throne with equal sincerity, and may any man who dares, say "I was a better man than he".'

I was born at Geneva in 1712, the son of Isaac Rousseau, a citizen of that town, and Susanne Bernard, his wife. My father's inheritance, being a fifteenth part only of a very small property, which had been divided among as many children, was almost nothing, and he relied for his living entirely on his trade of watchmaker, at which he was very highly skilled. My mother was the daughter of a minister of religion and rather better-off. She had beside both intelligence and beauty, and my father had not found it easy to win her. Their love had begun almost with their birth; at eight or nine they would walk together every evening along La Treille, and at ten they were inseparable. Sympathy and mental affinity strengthened in them a feeling first formed by habit. Both, being affectionate and sensitive by nature, were only waiting for the moment when they would find similar qualities in another; or rather the moment was waiting for them, and both threw their affections at the first heart that opened to receive them. Fate, by appearing to oppose their passion, only strengthened it. Unable to obtain his mistress, the young lover ate out his heart with grief, and she counselled him to travel and forget her. He travelled in vain, and returned more in love than ever, to find her he loved still faithful and fond. After such a proof, it was inevitable that they should love one another for all their lives. They swore to do so, and Heaven smiled on their vows.

Gabriel Bernard, one of my mother's brothers, fell in love with one of my father's sisters, and she refused to marry him unless her brother could marry my mother at the same time. Love overcame all obstacles, and the two pairs were wedded on the same day. So it was that my aunt married my uncle, and their children became my double first cousins. Within a year both couples had a child, but at the end of that time each of them was forced to separate.

My uncle Bernard, who was an engineer, went to serve in the Empire and Hungary under Prince Eugène, and distinguished himself at the siege and battle of Belgrade. My father, after the birth of my only brother, left for Constantinople, where he had been called to become watchmaker to the Sultan's Seraglio. While he was away my mother's beauty, wit, and talents brought her admirers, one of the most pressing of whom was M. de la Closure, the French Resident in the city. His feeling must have been very strong, for thirty years later I have seen him moved when merely speaking to me about her. But my mother had more than her virtue with which to defend herself; she deeply loved my father, and urged him to come back. He threw up everything to do so, and I was the unhappy fruit of his return. For ten months later I was born, a poor and sickly child, and cost my mother her life. So my birth was the first of my misfortunes.

I never knew how my father stood up to his loss, but I know that he never got over it. He seemed to see her again in me, but could never forget that I had robbed him of her; he never kissed me that I did not know by his sighs and his convulsive embrace that there was a bitter grief mingled with his affection, a grief which nevertheless intensified his feeling for me. When he said to me, 'Jean-Jacques, let us talk of your mother,' I would reply: 'Very well, father, but we are sure to cry.' 'Ah,' he would say with a groan, 'Give her back to me, console me for her, fill the void she has left in my heart! Should I love you so if you were not more to me than a son?' Forty years after he lost her he died in the arms of a second wife, but with his first wife's name on his lips and her picture imprinted upon his heart.

Such were my parents. And of all the gifts with which Heaven endowed them, they left me but one, a sensitive heart. It had been the making of their happiness, but for me it has been the cause of all the misfortunes in my life.

I was almost born dead, and they had little hope of saving me. I brought with me the seed of a disorder which has grown stronger with the years, and now gives me only occasional intervals of relief in which to suffer more painfully in some other way. But one of my father's sisters, a nice sensible woman, bestowed such care on me that I survived; and now, as I write this, she is still alive at the age of eighty, nursing a husband rather younger than herself but ruined by drink. My dear aunt, I pardon you for causing me to live, and I deeply regret that I cannot repay you in the evening of your days all the care and affection you lavished on me at the dawn of mine. My nurse Jacqueline is still alive too, healthy and strong. Indeed the fingers that opened my eyes at birth may well close them at my death.

I suffered before I began to think: which is the common fate of man, though crueller in my case than in another's. I know nothing of myself till I was five or six. I do not know how I learnt to read. I only remember my first books and their effect upon me; it is from my earliest reading that I date the unbroken consciousness of my own existence. My mother had possessed some novels, and my father and I began to read them after our supper. At first it was only to give me some practice in reading. But soon my interest in this entertaining literature became so strong that we read by turns continuously, and spent whole nights so engaged. For we could never leave off till the end of the book. Sometimes my father would say with shame as we heard the morning larks: 'Come, let us go to bed! I am more of a child than you are.'

In a short time I acquired by this dangerous method, not only an extreme facility in reading and expressing myself, but a singular insight for my age into the passions. I had no idea of the facts, but I was already familiar with every feeling. I had grasped nothing; I had sensed everything. These confused emotions which I experienced one after another, did not warp my reasoning powers in any way, for as yet I had none. But they shaped them after a special pattern, giving me the strangest and most romantic notions about human life, which neither experience nor reflection has ever succeeded in curing me of.

The novels gave out in the summer of 1719, and that winter we changed our reading. Having exhausted my mother's library, we turned to that portion of her father's which had fallen to us. Fortunately it contained some good books, as it could hardly fail to do, for the collection had been formed by a minister, who deserved the title, a man of learning, after the fashion of his day, but of taste and good sense as well. Lesueur's *History of Church and Empire*, Bossuet's *Discourse upon Universal History*, Plutarch's *Lives*, Nani's *History of Venice*, Ovid's *Metamorphoses*, La Bruyère,

Fontenelle's *Worlds* and his *Dialogues with the Dead*, and some volumes of Molière were transported to my father's workshop, where I read them to him every day while he worked.

Thus I acquired a sound taste, which was perhaps unique for my years. Plutarch, of them all, was my especial favourite, and the pleasure I took in reading and re-reading him did something to cure me of my passion for novels. Soon indeed I came to prefer Agesilaus, Brutus, and Aristides to Orondates, Artamenes, and Juba. It was this enthralling reading, and the discussions it gave rise to between my father and myself, that created in me that proud and intractable spirit, that impatience with the yoke of servitude, which has afflicted me throughout my life, in those situations least fitted to afford it scope. Continuously preoccupied with Rome and Athens, living as one might say with their great men, myself born the citizen of a republic and the son of a father whose patriotism was his strongest passion, I took fire by his example and pictured myself as a Greek or a Roman. I became indeed that character whose life I was reading; the recital of his constancy or his daring deeds so carrying me away that my eyes sparkled and my voice rang. One day when I was reading the story of Scaevola over table, I frightened them all by putting out my hand and grasping a chafing-dish in imitation of that hero.

I had one brother seven years older than myself, who was learning my father's trade. The extraordinary affection lavished upon me led to his being somewhat neglected, which I consider very wrong. Moreover his education had suffered by this neglect, and he was acquiring low habits even before he arrived at an age at which he could in fact indulge them. He was apprenticed to another master, with whom he took the same liberties as he had taken at home. I hardly ever saw him. Indeed, I can hardly say that I ever knew him, but I did not cease to love him dearly, and he loved me as well as a scoundrel can love. I remember once when my father was correcting him severely and angrily, throwing myself impetuously between them, and clasping my arms tightly around him. Thus I covered him with my body, and received the blows intended for him. So obstinately did I maintain my hold that, either as a result of my tearful cries or so as not to hurt me more than him, my father let him off his punishment. In the end my brother became so bad that he ran away and completely disappeared. We heard some time later that he was in Germany. But he did not write at all, and we had no more news of him after that. So it was that I became an only son.

But if that poor lad's upbringing was neglected, it was a different matter with his brother. No royal child could be more scrupulously cared for than I was in my early years. I was idolized by everyone around me, and what is rarer, always treated as a beloved son, never as a spoiled child. Never once, until I left my father's house, was I allowed to run out alone into the road with the other children. They never had to repress or to indulge in me any of those wayward humours that are usually attributed to Nature, but which are all the product of education alone. I had the faults of my years. I was a chatterer, I was greedy, and sometimes I lied. I would have stolen fruit or sweets or any kind of eatable; but I never took delight in being naughty or destructive, or in accusing other people or torturing poor animals. However, I do remember once having made water in one of our neighbour's cooking-pots while she was at church; her name was Mme Clot. I will even admit that the thought of it still makes me laugh, because Mme Clot, although a good woman on the whole, was the grumpiest old body I have ever met. And that is a brief and truthful account of all my childish misdeeds.

How could I have turned out wicked when I had nothing but examples of kindliness before my eyes, none but the best people in the world around me? My father, my aunt, my nurse, our friends and relations and everyone near me, may not have done my every bidding, but they did love me, and I loved them in return. My desires were so rarely excited and so rarely thwarted, that it never came into my head to have any. I could swear indeed that until I was put under a master I did not so much as know what it was to want my own way. When I was not reading or writing with my father, or going out for walks with my nurse, I spent all my time with my aunt, watching her embroider, hearing her sing, always sitting or standing beside her; and I was happy. Her cheerfulness and kindness and her pleasant face have left such an impression upon me that I can still remember her manner, her attitude and the way she looked. I recall too her affectionate little remarks, and I could still describe her clothes and her headdress, not forgetting the two curls of black hair she combed over her temples in the fashion of the day.

I am quite sure that it is to her I owe my taste, or rather my passion, for music, though it did not develop in me till long afterwards. She knew an enormous number of songs and tunes which she sang in a thin voice, that was very sweet. Such was the serenity of this excellent woman that it kept melancholy and sadness away, not only from her but from anyone who came near her; and such delight did I take in her singing that not only have many of her songs remained in my memory, but even now that I have lost her, others which I had completely forgotten since my childhood come back to me as I grow older, with a charm that I cannot express. It may seem incredible but, old dotard that I am, eaten up with cares and infirmities, I still find myself weeping like a child as I hum her little airs in my broken, tremulous voice. There is one in particular, the whole tune of which has come back to me. But the second half of the words persistently defies all my efforts to remember them, though I have a confused memory of the rhymes. Here is the opening and as much as I can recall of the rest:

> Thyrsis, I dare not come
> To listen to your playing
> Under the elm.
> For round our farm
> Do you know what they're saying?
>
> A shepherd born
> Who faithfully swore
> nothing to fear
> But never is a rose without a thorn.

I strive in vain to account for the strange effect which that song has on my heart, but I cannot explain why I am moved. All I know is that I am quite incapable of singing it to the end without breaking into tears. Countless times I have made up my mind to write to Paris and find out the rest of the words, if there is anyone who still knows them. But I am almost sure that the pleasure I derive from recalling the tune would partly vanish, once I had proof that anyone but my poor aunt Suson had sung it.

Such were the first affections of my dawning years; and thus there began to form in me, or to display itself for the first time, a heart at once proud and affectionate, and a character at once effeminate and inflexible, which by always wavering between weakness and courage, between self-indulgence and virtue, has throughout my life set me in conflict with myself, to such effect that abstinence and enjoyment, pleasure and prudence have alike eluded me.

The course of my education was interrupted by an accident, the consequences of which have influenced the rest of my life. My father quarrelled with M Gautier, a French captain with relations on the Council. This Gautier was a braggart and a coward who, happening to bleed at the nose, revenged himself by accusing my father of having drawn his sword against him in the city. When they decided to put my father in prison, however, he insisted that, according to the law, his accuser should be arrested also; and when he failed to get his way he preferred to leave Geneva and remain abroad for the rest of his life rather than lose both liberty and honour by giving in.

I stayed behind in the charge of my uncle Bernard, who was then employed on the city's fortifications. His elder daughter was dead, but he had a son of my age, and we were sent together to Bossey to board with the pastor, M. Lambercier, to learn Latin and all that sorry nonsense as well that goes by the name of education.

Two years' sojourn in that village somewhat modified my harsh Roman manners, and brought me back to the stage of childhood. At Geneva, where nothing was demanded of me, I loved steady reading, which was almost my sole amusement; at Bossey the work I had to do made me prefer games, which I played as a relaxation. The country too was such a fresh experience that I could never have enough of it. Indeed the taste that I got for it was so strong that it has remained inextinguishable, and the memory of the happy days I spent there has made me long regretfully for a country life and its pleasures at every stage of my existence, till now, when I am in the country once more. M. Lambercier was a very intelligent man; though he did not neglect our lessons, he did not load us with excessive work; and the proof of his capability is that, despite my dislike for compulsion, I have never looked back with distaste on my lesson times with him. I may not have learnt very much from him, but what I did learn I learnt without difficulty and I have remembered it all.

The simplicity of this rural existence brought me one invaluable benefit; it opened my heart to friendship. Up to that time I had known nothing but lofty and theoretical emotions. Living peacefully side by side with my cousin Bernard gave me a bond of affection with him, and in a very short time I felt a greater attachment for him than I had ever felt for my brother, an attachment that has never disappeared. He was a tall, lank, sickly boy, as mild in spirit as he was weak in body, and he never abused his favoured position in the house as my guardian's son. We shared the same studies, the same amusements, and the same tastes; we were on our own and of the same age; and each of us needed a companion; to be separated would have broken our hearts. Seldom though we had the opportunity of proving our attachment to one another, it was extremely strong. For not only could we not have lived one moment apart, but we never imagined that we could ever be parted. Being both of a nature easily swayed by affection, and tractable so long as there was no attempt at constraint, we were always in agreement on all subjects, and if the favour of our guardians gave him some advantage when they were present, the ascendancy was mine when we were alone – which redressed the balance. At our lessons I prompted him if he broke down; and when I had written my exercise I helped him with his. In our sports too I was the more active, and always took the lead. In fact our two natures agreed so well, and our friendship was so mutual and whole-hearted that for five complete years, both at Bossey and at Geneva, we were almost inseparable. We often fought, I confess, but no one ever had to part us. Not one of our quarrels lasted more than a quarter of an hour, and not once did either of us complain of the other. It may be said that these observations are puerile, but the relationship they describe is perhaps a unique one in all the history of childhood.

The manner of my life at Bossey suited me so well that if only it had lasted longer it could not have failed to fix my character for ever. It was founded on the affectionate, tender, and peaceable emotions. There was never, I believe, a creature of our kind with less vanity than I. By sudden transports I achieved moments of bliss, but immediately afterwards I relapsed into languuour. My strongest desire was to be loved by everyone who came near me. I was gentle, so was my cousin, and so were our guardians. For a whole two years I was neither the witness nor the victim of any violence. Everything served to strengthen the natural disposition of my heart. Nothing seemed to me so delightful as to see everyone pleased with me and with everything. I shall always remember repeating my catechism in church, where nothing upset me more than the grieved and anxious look on Mlle Lambercier's face when I hesitated. This made me unhappier than did my shame at faltering in public, though that too distressed me exceedingly. For although I was not very susceptible to praise, I was always extremely sensitive to disgrace. But I may say now that the expectation of a scolding from Mlle Lambercier alarmed me less than the fear of annoying her.

Neither she nor her brother was lacking in severity when

necessary. But as their severity was almost always just and never excessive, I took it to heart and never resented it. I was more upset at displeasing them, however, than at being punished; and a word of rebuke was more painful to me than a blow. It embarrasses me to be more explicit, but it is necessary nevertheless. How differently people would treat children if only they saw the eventual results of the indiscriminate, and often culpable, methods of punishment they employ! The magnitude of the lesson to be derived from so common and unfortunate a case as my own has resolved me to write it down.

Since Mlle Lambercier treated us with a mother's love, she had also a mother's authority, which she exercised sometimes by inflicting on us such childish chastisements as we had earned. For a long while she confined herself to threats, and the threat of a punishment entirely unknown to me frightened me sufficiently. But when in the end I was beaten I found the experience less dreadful in fact than in anticipation; and the very strange thing was that this punishment increased my affection for the inflicter. It required all the strength of my devotion and all my natural gentleness to prevent my deliberately earning another beating; I had discovered in the shame and pain of the punishment an admixture of sensuality which had left me rather eager than otherwise for a repetition by the same hand. No doubt, there being some degree of precocious sexuality in all this, the same punishment at the hands of her brother would not have seemed pleasant at all. But he was of too kindly a disposition to be likely to take over this duty; and so, if I refrained from earning a fresh punishment, it was only out of fear of annoying Mlle Lambercier; so much am I swayed by kindness, even by kindness that is based on sensuality, that it has always prevailed with me over sensuality itself.

The next occasion, which I postponed, although not through fear, occurred through no fault of mine – that is to say I did not act deliberately. But I may say that I took advantage of it with an easy conscience. The second occasion, however, was also the last. For Mlle Lambercier had no doubt detected signs that this punishment was not having the desired effect. She announced, therefore, that she would abandon it, since she found it too exhausting. Hitherto we had always slept in her room, and sometimes, in winter, in her bed. Two days afterwards we were made to sleep in another room, and henceforward I had the honour, willingly though I would have dispensed with it, of being treated as a big boy.

Who could have supposed that this childish punishment, received at the age of eight at the hands of a woman of thirty, would determine my tastes and desires, my passions, my very self for the rest of my life, and that in a sense diametrically opposed to the one in which they should normally have developed. At the moment when my senses were aroused my desires took a false turn and, confining themselves to this early experience, never set about seeking a different one. With sensuality burning in my blood almost from my birth, I kept myself pure and unsullied up to an age when even the coldest and most backward natures have developed. Tormented for a long while by I knew not what, I feasted feverish eyes on lovely women, recalling them ceaselessly to my imagination, but only to make use of them in my own fashion as so many Mlle Lamberciers.

3. William Wordsworth: *The Prelude*

Wordsworth (1770–1850) was born at Cockermouth, Cumberland, the son of a law agent. In 1792 he found himself in sympathy with the French Revolution but later, as it turned into the Terror, he became pessimistic about political revolution. With his friend, S. T. Coleridge, he published in 1798 *The Lyrical Ballads*, the poetic manifesto of the Romantic Movement. In 1799 he settled with his sister at Grasmere, where he spent the remainder of his life.

The Prelude, described by Wordsworth as 'a long poem upon the formation of my own mind' and dedicated to Coleridge, was begun somewhere in 1798 and completed in 1805 (a revised edition was published in 1850). Wordsworth's comments on *The Prelude* reveal its autobiographical intentions:

'Several years ago when the author retired to his native mountains with the hope of being enabled to construct a literary work that might live, it was a reasonable thing that he should take a review of his own mind, and examine how far Nature and Education had qualified him for such an employment. As subsidiary to this preparation, he undertook to record in verse, the origin and progress of his own powers as far as he was acquainted with them.'

Fair seed-time had my soul, and I grew up
Fostered alike by beauty and by fear:

Much favoured in my birthplace, and no less
In that belovèd Vale to which ere long
I was transplanted. Well I call to mind
('Twas at an early age, ere I had seen
Nine summers) when upon the mountain slope
The frost, and breath of frosty wind, had snapped
The last autumnal crocus, 'twas my joy
To wander half the night among the cliffs
And the smooth hollows where the woodcocks ran
Along the open turf. In thought and wish
That time, my shoulder all with springes hung,
I was a fell destroyer. On the heights
Scudding away from snare to snare, I plied
My anxious visitation, hurrying on,
Still hurrying, hurrying onward; – moon and stars
Were shining o'er my head. I was alone,
And seemed to be a trouble to the peace
That was among them. Sometimes it befell
In these night wanderings, that a strong desire
O'erpowered my better reason, and the bird
Which was the captive of another's toils
Became my prey; and when the deed was done
I heard among the solitary hills
Low breathings coming after me, and sounds
Of indistinguishable motion, steps
Almost as silent as the turf they trod.

Nor less in springtime when on southern banks
The shining sun had from his knot of leaves
Decoyed the primrose flower, and when the Vales
And woods were warm, was I a plunderer then
In the high places, on the lonesome peaks
Where'er, among the mountains and the winds,
The mother-bird had built her lodge; though mean
My object and inglorious, yet the end
Was not ignoble Oh! when I have hung
Above the raven's nest, by knots of grass
And half-inch fissures in the slippery rock
But ill-sustained, and almost (as it seemed)
Suspended by the blast which blew amain,
Shouldering the naked crag, oh, at that time
While on the perilous ridge I hung alone,

With what strange utterance did the loud dry wind
Blow through my ears! the sky seemed not a sky
Of earth – and with what motion moved the clouds!

The mind of man is framed even like the breath
And harmony of music; there is a dark
Invisible workmanship that reconciles
Discordant elements, and makes them move
In one society. Ah me! that all
The terrors, all the early miseries,
Regrets, vexations, lassitudes, that all
The thoughts and feelings which have been infused
Into my mind, should ever have made up
The calm existence that is mine when I
Am worthy of myself! Praise to the end!
Thanks likewise for the means! But I believe
That Nature, oftentimes, when she would frame
A favoured being, from his earliest dawn
Of infancy doth open out the clouds,
As at the touch of lightning, seeking him
With gentlest visitation; not the less,
Though haply aiming at the self-same end,
Does it delight her sometimes to employ
Severer interventions, ministry
More palpable, and so she dealt with me.

One evening (surely I was led by her)
I went alone into a shepherd's boat,
A skiff that to a willow tree was tied
Within a rocky cave, its usual home.
'Twas by the shores of Petterdale, a vale
Wherein I was a stranger, thither come
A schoolboy traveller, at the holidays.
Forth rambled from the village inn alone,
No sooner had I sight of this small skiff,
Discovered thus by unexpected chance,
Than I unloosed her tether and embarked.
The moon was up, the lake was shining clear
Among the hoary mountains; from the shore
I pushed, and struck the oars and struck again
In cadence and my little boat moved on,
Even like a man who walks with stately step

Though bent on speed. It was an act of stealth
And troubled pleasure, not without the voice
Of mountain-echoes did my boat move on;
Leaving behind her still, on either side,
Small circles glittering idly in the moon,
Until they melted all into one track
Of sparkling light. A rocky steep uprose
Above the cavern of the willow tree,
And now, as suited one who proudly rowed
With his best skill, I fixed a steady view
Upon the top of that same craggy ridge,
The bound of the horizon, for behind
Was nothing but the stars and the grey sky.
She was an elfin pinnace; lustily
I dipped my oars into the silent lake,
And, as I rose upon the stroke, my boat
Went heaving through the water like a swan;
When, from behind that craggy steep till then
The bound of the horizon, a huge cliff,
As if with voluntary power instinct,
Upreared its head. I struck and struck again,
And growing still in stature the huge cliff
Rose up between me and the stars, and still,
With measured motion, like a living thing,
Strode after me. With trembling hands I turned,
And through the silent water stole my way
Back to the cavern of the willow tree;
There in her mooring-place I left my bark, –
And through the meadows homeward went with grave
And serious thoughts; and after I had seen
That spectacle, for many days, my brain
Worked with a dim and undetermined sense
Of unknown modes of being; in my thoughts
There was a darkness, call it solitude
Or blank desertion. No familiar shapes
Of hourly objects, images of trees,
Of sea or sky, no colours of green fields;
But huge and mighty forms, that do not live
Like living men, moved slowly through my mind
By day, and were the trouble of my dreams.

Wisdom and Spirit of the universe!

Thou Soul that art the eternity of thought,
That giv'st to forms and images a breath
And everlasting motion, not in vain
By day or star-light thus from my first dawn
Of childhood didst thou intertwine for me
The passions that build up our human soul;
Not with the mean and vulgar works of man,
But with high objects, with enduring things –
With life and Nature, purifying thus
The elements of feeling and of thought,
And sanctifying, by such discipline,
Both pain and fear, until we recognize
A grandeur in the beatings of the heart.
Nor was this fellowship vouchsafed to me
With stinted kindness. In November days,
When vapours rolling down the valleys made
A lonely scene more lonesome, among woods
At noon, and 'mid the calm of summer nights,
When, by the margin of the trembling lake,
Beneath the gloomy hills I homeward went
In solitude, such intercourse was mine;
'Twas mine among the fields both day and night,
And by the waters, all the summer long.

And in the frosty season, when the sun
Was set, and visible for many a mile
The cottage windows through the twilight blazed,
I heeded not the summons: happy time
It was indeed for all of us – to me
It was a time of rapture! Clear and loud
The village clock tolled six, – I wheeled about,
Proud and exulting like an untired horse
That cares not for its home. All shod with steel,
We hissed along the polished ice in games
Confederate, imitative of the chase
And woodland pleasures, – the resounding horn,
The pack loud bellowing, and the hunted hare.
So through the darkness and the cold we flew,
And not a voice was idle; with the din,
Meanwhile, the precipices rang aloud;
The leafless trees and every icy crag
Tinkled like iron; while the distant hills

Into the tumult sent an alien sound
Of melancholy not unnoticed, while the stars
Eastward were sparkling clear, and in the west
The orange sky of evening died away.
Not seldom from the uproar I retired
Into a silent bay, or sportively
Glanced sideway, leaving the tumultuous throng,
To cut across the image of a star
That gleamed upon the ice; and oftentimes,
When we had given our bodies to the wind,
And all the shadowy banks on either side
Came sweeping through the darkness, spinning still
The rapid line of motion, then at once
Have I, reclining back upon my heels,
Stopped short; yet still the solitary cliffs
Wheeled by me – even as if the earth had rolled
With visible motion her diurnal round!
Behind me did they stretch in solemn train,
Feebler and feebler, and I stood and watched
Till all was tranquil as a dreamless sleep.

 Ye Presences of Nature in the sky
Or on the earth! Ye Visions of the hills!
And Souls of lonely places! can I think
A vulgar hope was yours when ye employed
Such ministry, when ye through many a year
Haunting me thus among my boyish sports,
On caves and trees, upon the woods and hills,
Impressed upon all forms the characters
Of danger or desire; and thus did make
The surface of the universal earth
With triumph and delight, and hope and fear,
Work like a sea?
    Not uselessly employed,
I might pursue this theme through every change
Of exercise and play, to which the year
Did summon us in its delightful round.

4. Samuel Taylor Coleridge:
Letters to Poole

Coleridge (1772–1834) was born at Ottery St Mary, Devonshire, the son of a minister. In 1794 he formulated, with Robert Southey and others, a scheme for an ideal community, but the plan collapsed in the following year. In 1817 he published *Biographia Literaria*, a rambling but seminal book on the nature of literature. He was responsible for introducing German Romantic and metaphysical ideas (from Kant and Schelling) into England and saw his mission, in much the same way as William Blake, as pitting the power of creative imagination against the mechanical and empirical theories of Locke, Hume and Hartley.

In 1797 he began writing a sequence of autobiographical letters to his friend Poole. 'What I am,' he wrote, 'Depends on what I have been.' These letters provide a vivid insight into the childhood of a man who sought in his adult life to articulate a vast and holy conception of life.

TO THOMAS POOLE

Monday, February, 1797

My Dear Poole,—I could inform the dullest author how he might write an interesting book. Let him relate the events of his own life with honesty, not disguising the feelings that accompanied them. I never yet read even a Methodist's Experience in the 'Gospel Magazine' without receiving instruction and amusement; and I should almost despair of that man who could peruse the 'Life of John Woolman' without an amelioration of heart. As to my Life, it has all the charms of variety—high life and low life, vices and virtues, great folly and some wisdom. However, what I am depends on what I have been; and you, *my best Friend!* have a right to the narration. To me the task will be a useful one. It will renew and deepen my reflections on the past; and it will perhaps make you behold with no unforgiving or impatient eye those weaknesses and defects in my character, which so many untoward circumstances have concurred to plant there. . . .

October 9, 1797

My dearest Poole,—From March to October—a long silence! But [as] it is possible that I may have been preparing materials for future letters the time cannot be considered as altogether subtracted from you.

From October, 1775, to October, 1778. These three years I continued at the Reading School, because I was too little to be trusted among my father's schoolboys. After breakfast I had a halfpenny given me, with which I bought three cakes at the baker's close by the school of my old mistress; and these were my dinner on every day except Saturday and Sunday; when I used to dine at home, and wallowed in a beef and pudding dinner. I am remarkably fond of beans and bacon; and this fondness I attribute to my father having given me a penny for having eat a large quantity of beans on Saturday. For the other boys did not like them, and as it was an economic food, my father thought that my attachment and penchant for it ought to be encouraged. My father was very fond of me, and I was my mother's darling: in consequence I was very miserable. For Molly, who had nursed my brother Francis, and was immoderately fond of him, hated me because my mother took more notice of me than of Frank, and Frank hated me because my mother gave me now and then a bit of cake, when he had none – quite forgetting that for one bit of cake which I had and he had not, he had twenty sops in the pan, and pieces of bread and butter with sugar on them from Molly, from whom I received only thumps and ill names.

So I became fretful and timorous, and a tell-tale; and the schoolboys drove me from play, and were always tormenting me, and hence I took no pleasure in boyish sports, but read incessantly. My father's sister kept an everything shop at Crediton, and there I read through all the gilt-cover little books that could be had at that time, and likewise all the uncovered tales of Tom Hickathrift, Jack the Giant Killer, etc, etc, etc. And I used to lie by the wall and mope, and my spirits used to come upon me suddenly; and in a flood of them I was accustomed to race up and down the churchyard, and act over all I had been reading, on the docks, the nettles, and the rank grass. At six years old I remember to have read Belisarius, Robinson Crusoe, and Philip Quarles; and then I found the Arabian Nights' Entertainments, one tale of which (the tale of a man who was compelled to seek for a pure virgin) made so deep an impression on me (I had read it in the evening while my mother was mending stockings), that I was haunted by spectres, whenever I was in the dark: and I distinctly remember the anxious and fearful eagerness with which I used to watch the window in which the books lay, and whenever the sun lay upon them, I would seize it, carry it by the wall, and bask and read. My father found out the effect which these books had produced, and burnt them.

So I became a dreamer, and acquired an indisposition to all bodily activity; and I was fretful and inordinately passionate, and as I could not play at anything, and was slothful, I was despised and hated by the boys; and because I could read and spell and had, I may truly say, a memory and understanding forced into almost an unnatural ripeness, I was flattered and wondered at by all the old women. And so I became very vain, and despised most of the boys that were at all near my own age, and before I was eight years old I was a character. Sensibility, imagination, vanity, sloth, and feelings of deep and bitter contempt for all who traversed the orbit of my understanding, were even then prominent and manifest.

From October, 1778, to 1779. That which I began to be from three to six I continued from six to nine. In this year (1778) I was admitted into the Grammar School, and soon outstripped all of my age. I had a dangerous putrid fever this year. My brother George lay ill of the same fever in the next room. My poor brother Francis, I remember, stole up in spite of orders to the contrary, and sat by my bedside and read Pope's Homer to me. Frank had a violent love of beating me; but whenever that was superseded by any humour or circumstances, he was always very fond of me and used to regard me with a strange mixture of admiration and contempt. Strange it was not, for he hated books, and loved climbing, fighting, playing and robbing orchards, to distraction.

My mother relates a story of me, which I repeat here, because it must be regarded as my first piece of wit. During my fever, I asked why Lady Northcote (our neighbour) did not come and see me. My mother said she was afraid of catching the fever. I was piqued and answered, 'Ah, Mamma! the four Angels round my bed an't afraid of catching it!' I suppose you know the prayer:—

> Matthew! Mark! Luke and John!
> God bless the bed which I lie on.
> Four angels round me spread,
> Two at my foot, and two at my head.

This prayer I said nightly, and most firmly believed the truth of it. Frequently I have (half-awake and half-asleep, my body diseased and fevered by my imagination) seen armies of ugly things bursting in upon me, and these four angels keeping them off. In my next I shall carry on my life to my father's death.

God bless you, my dear Poole, and your affectionate

S. T. COLERIDGE

October 16, 1797

Dear Poole, From October, 1779, to October 1781. I had asked my mother one evening to cut my cheese entire, so that I might toast it. This was no easy matter, it being a *crumbly* cheese. My mother, however, did it. I went into the garden for something or other, and in the mean time my brother Frank *minced* my cheese 'to disappoint the favourite'. I returned, saw the exploit, and in an agony of passion flew at Frank. He pretended to have been seriously hurt by my blow, flung himself on the ground, and there lay with outstretched limbs. I hung over him moaning, and in a great fright; he leaped up, and with a horse-laugh gave me a severe blow in the face. I seized a knife and was running at him, when my mother came in and took me by the arm. I expected a flogging, and struggling from her I ran away to a hill at the bottom of which the Otter flows, about one mile from Ottery. There I stayed; my rage died away, but my obstinacy vanquished my fears, and taking out a little shilling book, which had, at the end, morning and evening prayers, I very devoutly repeated them – thinking at the *same time* with inward and gloomy satis-faction how miserable my mother must be! I distinctly remember my feelings when I saw a Mr Vaughan pass over the bridge, at about a furlong's distance, and how I watched the calves in the fields beyond the river. It grew dark and I fell asleep. It was towards the latter end of October, and it proved a dreadful stormy night. I felt the cold in my sleep, and dreamt that I was pulling the blanket over me, and actually pulled over me a dry thorn bush which lay on the hill. In my sleep I had rolled from the top of the hill to within three yards of the river, which flowed by the unfenced edge at the bottom. I awoke several times, and finding myself wet and stiff and cold, closed my eyes again that I might forget it.

In the meantime my mother waited about half an hour, expecting my return when the *sulks* had evaporated. I not return-ing, she sent into the churchyard and round the town. Not found! Several men and all the boys were sent to ramble about and seek me. In vain! My mother was almost distracted; and at ten o'clock at night I was *cried* by the crier in Ottery, and in two villages near it, with a reward offered for me. No one went to bed; indeed, I believe half the town were up all the night. To return to myself. About five in the morning, or a little after, I was broad awake, and attempted to get up and walk; but I could not move. I saw the shepherds and workmen at a distance, and cried, but so faintly that it was impossible to hear me thirty yards off. And there I might have lain and died; for I was now almost given over, the ponds and even the river, near where I was lying, having been dragged. But by good luck, Sir Stafford Northcote, who had been out all night, resolved to make one other trial, and came so near that he heard me crying. He carried me in his arms for near a quarter of a mile, when we met my father and Sir Stafford's servants. I remember and never shall forget my father's face as he looked upon me while I lay in the servant's arms – so calm, and the tears stealing down his face; for I was the child of his old age. My mother, as you may suppose, was outrageous with joy. (Meantime) in rushed a *young lady*, crying out, 'I hope you'll whip him, Mrs Coleridge!' This woman still lives in Ottery; and neither philosophy or religion have been able to conquer the antipathy which I feel towards her whenever I see her. I was put to bed and recovered in a day or so, but I was certainly injured. For I was weakly and subject to the ague for many years after.

My father (who had so little of parental ambition in him, that he had destined his children to be blacksmiths &c., and had accomplished his intention but for my mother's pride and spirit of aggrandizing her family) – my father had, however, resolved that I should be a parson. I read every book that came in my way without distinction; and my father was fond of me, and used to take me on his knee and hold long conversations with me. I remember that at eight years old I walked with him one winter evening from a farmer's house a mile from Ottery, and he told me the names of the stars and how Jupiter was a thousand times larger than our world, and that the other twinkling stars were suns that had worlds rolling round them; and when I came home he shewed me how they rolled round. I heard him with a profound delight and admiration: but without the least mixture of wonder or incredulity. For from my early reading of fairy tales and genii, etc., etc., my mind had been habituated to the Vast, and I never regarded my senses in any way as the criteria of my belief. I regulated all my creeds by my conceptions, not by my sight, even at that age. Should children be permitted to read romances, and relations of giants and magicians and genii? I know all that has been said against it; but I have formed my faith in the affirmative. I know no other way of giving the mind a love of the Great and the Whole. Those who have been led to the same truths step by step, through the constant testimony of their senses, seem to me to want a sense which I possess. They contemplate nothing but parts, and all parts are necessarily little. And the universe to them is but a mass of little things. It is true, that the mind may become credulous and prone to superstition by the former method; but are not the experimentalists credulous even to madness in believing any absurdity, rather than believe the grandest truths, if they have not the testimony of their own senses in their favour? I have known some who have been rationally educated, as it is styled. They were marked by a microscopic acuteness, but when they looked at great things, all became a blank and they saw nothing, and denied (very illogically) that anything could be seen, and uniformly put the negation of a power for the possession of a power, and called the want of imagination judgement and the never being moved to rapture philosophy!

Towards the latter end of September, 1781, my father went to Plymouth with my brother Francis, who was to go as midshipman under Admiral Graves who was a friend of my father's. My father settled my brother, and returned October 4, 1781. He arrived at Exeter about six o'clock, and was pressed to take a bed there at the Harts', but he refused and, to avoid their entreaties, he told them, that he had never been superstitious, but that the night before he had had a dream which had made a deep impression. He dreamt that Death had appeared to him as he is commonly painted, and touched him with his dart. Well, he returned home, and all his family, I excepted, were up. He told my mother his dream; he was in high health and good spirits, and there was a bowl of punch made, and my father gave a long and particular account of his travel, and that he had placed Frank under a religious captain, &c. At length he went to bed, very well and in high spirits. A short time after he had lain down he complained of a pain in his bowels. My mother got him some peppermint water, and, after a pause, he said 'I am much better now, my dear!' and lay down again. In a minute my mother heard a noise in his throat, and spoke to him, but he did not answer; and she spoke repeatedly in vain. Her *shriek* awaked me, and I said 'Papa is dead!' I did not know of my father's return, but I knew that he was expected. How I came to think of his death I cannot tell but it was so. Dead he was. Some said it was the gout in the heart; – probably it was a fit of apoplexy. He was an Israelite without guile, simple, generous, and taking some Scriptural texts in their literal sense, he was conscientiously indifferent to the good and the evil of this world.

God love you and

S. T. COLERIDGE

5. John Stuart Mill: *Autobiography*

John Stuart Mill (1806–73) was the son of James Mill – a follower of the philosopher, Jeremy Bentham, and the economist, Ricardo. In 1861 he founded *The Utilitarian Society* and 1861 published *Utilitarianism*. He was also the author of *System of Logic*, *Principles of Political Economy*, *Liberty*, and *The Subjection of Women*.

He wrote his autobiography between 1853 and 1856. The main interest of the autobiography lies in Mill's description and evaluation of his education, which was completely determined by his father, and the crisis which it led to in his subsequent life. John Stuart Mill claimed that his father's training, ignoring the inward culture of the individual, had all but destroyed his capacity to feel. Mill, it will be remembered, was taught Greek at the age of three, Latin at the age of seven, Logic at twelve and Political Economy at thirteen. 'I started,' claimed Mill in his autobiography, ' I may fairly say, with an advantage of a quarter of a century over my contemporaries.' But, at the same time, it led him at twenty, to contemplate suicide, so blank and devoid of feeling had his life become. It was the discovery of poetry – in particular the poetry of Wordsworth and Coleridge – that released the suppressed springs of feeling and introduced Mill to a richer and deeper understanding of existence.

From the winter of 1821, when I first read Bentham, and especially from the commencement of the *Westminster Review*, I had what might truly be called an object in life; to be a reformer of the world. My conception of my own happiness was entirely identified with this object. The personal sympathies I wished for were those of fellow labourers in this enterprise. I endeavoured to pick up as many flowers as I could by the way; but as a serious and permanent personal satisfaction to rest upon, my whole reliance was placed on this; and I was accustomed to felicitate myself on the certainty of a happy life which I enjoyed, through placing my happiness in something durable and distant, in which some progress might be always making, while it could never be exhausted by complete attainment. This did very well for several years, during which the general improvement going on in the world and the idea of myself as engaged with others in struggling to promote it, seemed enough to fill up an interesting and animated existence. But the time came when I awakened from this as from a dream. It was in the autumn of 1826. I was in a dull state of nerves, such as everybody is occasionally liable to; unsusceptible to enjoyment or pleasurable excitement; one of those moods when what is pleasure at other times becomes insipid or indifferent; the state, I should think, in which converts to Methodism usually are, when smitten by their first 'conviction of sin'. In this frame of mind it occurred to me to put the question directly to myself: 'Suppose that all your objects in life were realized; that all the changes in institutions and opinions which you are looking forward to, could be completely effected at this very instant: would this be a great joy and happiness to you?' And an irrepressible self-consciousness distinctly answered, 'No!' At this my heart sank within me: the whole foundation on which my life was constructed fell down. All my happiness was to have been found in the continual pursuit of this end. The end had ceased to charm, and how could there ever again be any interest in the means? I seemed to have nothing left to live for.

At first I hoped that the cloud would pass away of itself; but it did not. A night's sleep, the sovereign remedy for the smaller vexations of life, had no effect on it. I awoke to a renewed consciousness of the woeful fact. I carried it with me into all companies, into all occupations. Hardly anything had power to cause me even a few minutes' oblivion of it. For some months the cloud seemed to grow thicker and thicker. The lines in Coleridge's 'Dejection'—I was not then acquainted with them—exactly describe my case:

> A grief without a pang, void, dark and drear,
> A drowsy, stifled, unimpassioned grief,
> Which finds no natural outlet or relief
> In word, or sigh, or tear.

In vain I sought relief from my favourite books; those memorials of past nobleness and greatness from which I had always hitherto drawn strength and animation. I read them now without feeling, or with the accustomed feeling *minus* all its charm; and I became persuaded that my love of mankind, and of excellence for its own sake, had worn itself out. I sought no comfort by speaking to others of what I felt. If I had loved any one sufficiently to make confiding my griefs a necessity, I should not have been in the condition I was. I felt, too, that mine was not an interesting, or in any way respectable distress. There was nothing in it to attract sympathy. Advice, if I had known where to seek it, would have been most precious. The words of Macbeth to the physician often occurred to my thoughts. But there was no one on whom I could build the faintest hope of such assistance. My father, to whom it would have been natural to me to have recourse in any practical difficulties, was the last person to whom, in such a case as this, I looked for help. Everything convinced me that he had no knowledge of any such mental state as I was suffering from, and that even if he could be made to understand it, he was not the physician who could heal it. My education, which was wholly his work, had been conducted without any regard to the possibility of its ending in this result; and I saw no use in giving him the pain of thinking that his plans had failed, when the failure was probably irremediable, and, at all events, beyond the power of *his* remedies. Of other friends I had at that time none to whom I had any hope of making my condition intelligible. It was however abundantly intelligible to myself; and the more I dwelt upon it, the more hopeless it appeared.

My course of study had led me to believe that all mental and moral feelings and qualities, whether of a good or of a bad kind, were the results of association; that we love one thing, and hate another, take pleasure in one sort of action or contemplation, and pain in another sort, through the clinging of pleasurable or painful ideas to those things, from the effect of education or of experience. As a corollary from this, I had always heard it maintained by my father, and was myself convinced, that the object of education should be to form the strongest possible associations of the salutary class; associations of pleasure with all things beneficial to the great whole, and of pain with all things hurtful to it. This doctrine appeared inexpugnable; but it now seemed to me, on retrospect, that my teachers had occupied themselves but superficially with the means of forming and keeping up these salutary associations. They seemed to have trusted altogether to the old familiar instruments, praise and blame, reward and punishment. Now, I did not doubt that by these means, begun early, and applied unremittingly, intense associations of pain and pleasure, especially of pain, might be created, and might produce desires and aversions capable of lasting undiminished to the end of life. But there must always be something artificial and casual in associations thus produced. The pains and pleasures thus forcibly associated with things are not connected with them by any natural tie; and it is therefore, I thought, essential to the durability of these associations, that they should have become so intense and inveterate as to be practically indissoluble before the habitual exercise of the power of analysis had commenced. For I now saw, or thought I saw, what I had always before received with incredulity—that the habit of analysis has a tendency to wear away the feelings; as indeed it has, when no other mental habit is cultivated, and the analysing spirit remains without its natural complements and correctives. The very excellence of analysis (I argued) is that it tends to weaken and undermine whatever is the result of prejudice; that it enables us mentally to separate ideas which have only casually clung together; and no associations whatever could ultimately resist this dissolving force, were it not that we owe to analysis our clearest knowledge of the permanent sequences in nature; the real connexions between things, not dependent on our will and feelings; natural laws, by virtue of which, in many cases, one thing is inseparable from another in fact; which laws, in proportion as they are clearly perceived and imaginatively realized, cause our ideas of things which are always joined together in Nature to cohere more and more closely in our thoughts. Analytic habits may thus even strengthen the associations between causes and effects, means and ends, but tend altogether to weaken those which are, to speak familiarly, a *mere* matter of feeling. They are therefore (I thought) favourable to prudence and clear-sightedness, but a perpetual worm at the root both of the passions and of the virtues; and, above all, fearfully undermine all desires, and all pleasures, which are the effects of association, that is, according to the theory I held, all except the purely physical and organic; of the entire insufficiency of which to make life desirable no one had a stronger conviction than I had. These were the laws of human nature, by which, as it seemed to me, I had been brought to my present state. All those to whom I looked up were of opinion that the pleasure of sympathy with human beings, and the feelings which made the good of others, and especially of mankind on a large scale, the object of existence, were the greatest and surest sources of happiness. Of the truth of this I was convinced, but to know that a feeling would make me happy if I had it, did not give me the feeling. My education, I thought, had failed to create these feelings in sufficient strength to resist the dissolving influences of analysis, while the whole course of my intellectual cultivation had made precocious and premature analysis the inveterate habit of my mind. I was thus, as I said to myself, left stranded at the commencement of my voyage, with a well-equipped ship and a rudder, but no sail; without any real desire for the ends which I had been so carefully fitted out to work for: no delight in virtue, or the general good, but also just as little in anything else. The fountains of vanity and ambition seemed to have dried up within me, as completely as those of benevolence. I had had (as I reflected) some gratification of vanity at too early an age: I had obtained some distinction, and felt myself of some importance, before the desire of distinction and of importance had grown into a passion; and little as it was which I had attained, yet having been attained too early, like all pleasures enjoyed too soon, it had made me blasé and indifferent to the pursuit. Thus neither selfish nor unselfish pleasures were pleasures to me. And there seemed no power in nature sufficient to begin the formation of my character anew, and create, in a mind now irretrievably analytic, fresh associations of pleasure with any of the objects of human desire.

These were the thoughts which mingled with the dry heavy dejection of the melancholy winter of 1826–1827. During this time I was not incapable of my usual occupations. I went on with them mechanically, by the mere force of habit. I had been so drilled in a certain sort of mental exercise that I could still carry it on when all the spirit had gone out of it. I even composed and spoke several speeches at the debating society, how, or with what degree of success, I know not. Of four years continual speaking at that society, this is the only year of which I remember next to nothing. Two lines of Coleridge, in whom alone of all writers I have found a true description of what I felt, were often in my thoughts, not at this time (for I had never read them), but in a later period of the same mental malady:

> Work without hope draws nectar in a sieve,
> And hope without an object cannot live.

In all probability my case was by no means so peculiar as I fancied it, and I doubt not that many others have passed through a similar state; but the idiosyncrasies of my education had given to the general phenomenon a special character, which made it seem the natural effect of causes that it was hardly possible for time to remove. I frequently asked myself, if I could, or if I was bound to go on living, when life must be passed in this manner. I generally answered to myself that I did not think I could possibly bear it beyond a year. When, however, not more than half that duration of time had elapsed, a small ray of light broke in upon my gloom. I was reading, accidentally, Marmontel's *Memoires*, and came to the passage which relates his father's death, the distressed position of the family, and the sudden inspiration by which he, then a mere boy, felt and made them feel that he would be everything to them—would supply the place of all that they had lost. A vivid conception of the scene and its feelings came over me, and I was moved to tears. From this moment my burden grew lighter. The oppression of the thought that all feeling was dead within me was gone. I was no longer hopeless: I was not a stock or a stone. I had still, it seemed, some of the material out of which all worth of character, and all capacity for happiness, are made. Relieved from my ever-present sense of irremediable wretchedness, I gradually found that the ordinary incidents of life could again give me some pleasure; that I could again find enjoyment, not intense, but sufficient for cheerfulness, in sunshine and sky, in books, in conversation, in public affairs; and that there was, once more, excitement, though of a moderate kind, in exerting myself for my opinions, and for the public good. Thus the cloud gradually drew off, and I again enjoyed life; and though I had several relapses, some of which lasted many months, I never again was as miserable as I had been.

The experiences of this period had two very marked effects on my opinions and character. In the first place, they led me to adopt a theory of life, very unlike that on which I had before acted, and having much in common with what at that time I certainly had never heard of, the anti-self-consciousness theory of Carlyle. I never, indeed, wavered in the conviction that happiness is the test of all rules of conduct, and the end of life. But I now thought that this end was only to be attained by not making it the direct end. Those only are happy (I thought) who have their minds fixed on some object other than their own happiness; on the happiness of others, on the improvement of mankind, even on some art or pursuit, followed not as a means, but as itself an ideal end. Aiming thus at something else, they find happiness

A.E.—3*

by the way. The enjoyments of life (such was now my theory) are sufficient to make it a pleasant thing, when they are taken *en passant*, without being made a principal object. Once make them so, and they are immediately felt to be insufficient. They will not bear a scrutinizing examination. Ask yourself whether you are happy, and you cease to be so. The only chance is to treat, not happiness, but some end external to it, as the purpose of life. Let your self-consciousness, your scrutiny, your self-interrogation, exhaust themselves on that; and if otherwise fortunately circumstanced, you will inhale happiness with the air you breathe, without dwelling on it or thinking about it, without either forestalling it in imagination, or putting it to flight by fatal questioning. This theory now became the basis of my philosophy of life. And I still hold to it as the best theory for all those who have but a moderate degree of sensibility and of capacity for enjoyment, that is, for the great majority of mankind.

The other important change which my opinions at this time underwent was that I, for the first time, gave its proper place, among the prime necessities of human well-being, to the internal culture of the individual. I ceased to attach almost exclusive importance to the ordering of outward circumstances, and the training of the human being for speculation and for action.

I had now learnt by experience that the passive susceptibilities needed to be cultivated as well as the active capacities, and required to be nourished and enriched as well as guided; I did not, for an instant, lose sight of, or undervalue, that part of the truth which I had seen before; I never turned recreant to intellectual culture, or ceased to consider the power and practice of analysis as an essential condition both of individual and of social improvement. But I thought that it had consequences which required to be corrected, by joining other kinds of cultivation with it. The maintenance of a due balance among the faculties now seemed to me of primary importance. The cultivation of the feelings became one of the cardinal points in my ethical and philosophical creed. And my thoughts and inclinations turned in an increasing degree towards whatever seemed capable of being instrumental to that object.

I now began to find meaning in the things which I had read or heard about the importance of poetry and art as instruments of human culture. But it was some time longer before I began to know this by personal experience. The only one of the imaginative arts in which I had from childhood taken great pleasure was music; the best effect of which (and in this it surpasses perhaps every other art) consists in exciting enthusiasm; in winding up to a high pitch those feelings of an elevated kind which are already in the character, but to which this excitement gives a glow and a fervour, which, though transitory at its utmost height, is precious for sustaining them at other times. This effect of music I had often experienced; but like all my pleasurable susceptibilities it was suspended during the gloomy period. I had sought relief again and again from this quarter, but found none. After the tide had turned, and I was in process of recovery, I had been helped forward by music, but in a much less elevated manner. I at this time first became acquainted with Weber's *Oberon*, and the extreme pleasure which I drew from its delicious melodies did me good, by showing me a source of pleasure to which I was as susceptible as ever. The good, however, was much impaired by the thought that the pleasure of music (as is quite true of such pleasure as this was, that of mere tune) fades with familiarity, and requires either to be revived by intermittence, or fed by continual novelty. And it is very characteristic both of my then state, and of the general tone of my mind at this point of my life, that I was seriously tormented by the thought of the exhaustibility of musical combinations. The octave consists only of five tones and two semitones, which can be put together in only a limited number of ways, of which but a small proportion are beautiful; most of these, it seemed to me, must have been already discovered, and there could not be room for a long succession of Mozarts and Webers to strike out, as these had done, entirely new and surpassingly rich veins of musical beauty. This source of anxiety may, perhaps, be thought to resemble that of the philosophers of Laputa, who feared lest the sun should be burnt out. It was, however, connected with the best feature in my character, and the only good point to be found in my very unromantic and in no way honourable distress. For though my dejection, honestly looked at, could not be called other than egotistical, produced by the ruin, as I thought, of my fabric of happiness, yet the destiny of mankind in general was ever in my thoughts, and could not be separated from my own. I felt that the flaw in my life must be a flaw in life itself; that the question was, whether, if the reformers of society and government could succeed in their objects, and every person in the community were free and in a state of physical comfort, the pleasures of life, being no longer kept up by struggle and privation, would cease to be pleasures. And I felt that unless I could see my way to some better hope than this for human happiness in general, my dejection must continue; but that if I could see such an outlet, I should then look on the world with pleasure; content, as far as I was myself concerned, with any fair share of the general lot.

This state of my thoughts and feelings made the fact of my reading Wordsworth for the first time (in the autumn of 1823), an important event in my life. I took up the collection of his poems from curiosity, with no expectation of mental relief from it, though I had before resorted to poetry with that hope. In the worst period of my depression, I had read through the whole of Byron (then new to me), to try whether a poet, whose peculiar department was supposed to be that of the intenser feelings, could rouse any feeling in me. As might be expected, I got no good from this reading, but the reverse. The poet's state of mind was too like my own. His was the lament of a man who had worn out all pleasures, and who seemed to think that life, to all who possess the good things of it, must necessarily be the vapid, uninteresting thing which I found it. His *Harold* and *Manfred* had the same burden on them which I had; and I was not in a frame of mind to desire any comfort from the vehement sensual passion of his Giaours, or the sullenness of his Laras. But while Byron was exactly what did not suit my condition, Wordsworth was exactly what did. I had looked into the *Excursion* two or three years before, and found little in it; and I should probably have found as little, had I read it at this time. But the miscellaneous poems, in the two-volume edition of 1815 (to which little of value was added in the latter part of the author's life), proved to be the precise thing for my mental wants at that particular juncture.

In the first place, these poems addressed themselves powerfully to one of the strongest of my pleasurable susceptibilities, the love of rural objects and natural scenery; to which I had been indebted not only for much of the pleasure of my life, but quite recently for relief from one of my longest relapses into depression. In this power of rural beauty over me, there was a foundation laid for taking pleasure in Wordsworth's poetry; the more so as his scenery lies mostly among mountains, which, owing to my early Pyrenean excursion, were my ideal of natural beauty. But Wordsworth would never have had any great effect on me if he had merely placed before me beautiful pictures of natural scenery. Scott does this still better than Wordsworth, and a very second-rate landscape does it more effectually than any poet. What made Wordsworth's poems a medicine for my state of mind was that they expressed not mere outward beauty, but states of feeling, and of thought coloured by feeling, under the excitement of beauty. They seemed to be the very culture of the feelings, which I was in quest of. In them I seemed to draw from a source of inward joy, of sympathetic and imaginative pleasure, which could be shared in by all human beings; which had no connexion with struggle or imperfection, but would be made richer by every improvement in the physical or social condition of mankind. From them I seemed to learn what would be the perennial sources of happiness when all the greater evils of life shall have been removed. And I felt myself at once better and happier as I came under their influence. There have certainly been, even in our own age, greater poets than Wordsworth; but poetry of deeper and loftier feeling could not have done for me at that time what his did. I needed to be made to feel that there was real, permanent happiness in tranquil contemplation. Wordsworth taught me this, not only without turning away from, but with a greatly increased interest in the common feelings and common destiny of human beings. And the delight which these poems gave me proved that with culture of this sort there was nothing to dread from the most confirmed habit of analysis. At the conclusion of the *Poems* came the famous ode, falsely called Platonic, 'Intimations of Immortality'; in which, along with more than his usual sweetness of melody and rhythm, and along with the two passages of grand imagery but bad philosophy so often quoted, I found that he too had had similar experience to mine; that he also had felt that the first freshness of youthful enjoyment of life was not lasting; but that he had sought for compensation, and found it, in the way in which he was now teaching me to find it. The result was that I gradually, but completely, emerged from my habitual depression, and was never again subject to it. I long continued to value Wordsworth less according to his intrinsic merits than by the measure of what he had done for me. Compared with the greatest poets, he may be said to be the poet of unpoetical natures, possessed of quiet and contemplative tastes. But unpoetical natures are precisely those which require poetic cultivation. This cultivation Wordsworth is much more fitted to give than poets who are intrinsically far more poets than he.

It so fell out that the merits of Wordsworth were the occasion of my first public declaration of my new way of thinking, and separation from those of my habitual companions who had not undergone a similar change. The person with whom at that time I was most in the habit of comparing notes on such subjects was Roebuck, and I induced him to read Wordsworth, in whom he also at first seemed to find much to admire; but I, like most Wordsworthians, threw myself into strong antagonism to Byron, both as a poet and as to his influence on the character. Roebuck, all whose instincts were those of action and struggle, had, on the contrary, a strong relish and great admiration of Byron, whose writings he regarded as the poetry of human life, while Wordsworth's, according to him, was that of flowers and butterflies. We agreed to have the fight out at our Debating Society, where we accordingly discussed for two evenings the comparative merits of Byron and Wordsworth, propounding and illustrating by long recitations our respective theories of poetry; Sterling also, in a brilliant speech, putting forward his particular theory. This was the first debate on any weighty subject in which Roebuck and I had been on opposite sides. The schism between us widened from this time more and more, though we continued for some years longer to be companions. In the beginning, our chief divergence related to the cultivation of the feelings. Roebuck was in many respects very different from the vulgar notion of a Benthamite or Utilitarian. He was a lover of poetry and of most of the fine arts. He took great pleasure in music, in dramatic performances, especially in painting, and himself drew and designed landscapes with great facility and beauty. But he never could be made to see that these things have any value as aids in the formation of character. Personally, instead of being, as Benthamites are supposed to be, void of feeling, he had very quick and strong sensibilities. But, like most Englishmen who have feelings, he found his feelings stand very much in his way. He was much more susceptible to the painful sympathies than to the pleasurable, and looking for his happiness elsewhere, he wished that his feelings should be deadened rather than quickened. And, in truth, the English character, and English social circumstances, make it so seldom possible to derive happiness from the exercise of the sympathies that it is not wonderful if they count for little in an Englishman's scheme of life. In most other countries the paramount importance of the sympathies as a constituent of individual happiness is an axiom, taken for granted rather than needing any formal statement; but most English thinkers seem to regard them as necessary evils, required for keeping men's actions benevolent and compassionate. Roebuck was, or appeared to be, this kind of Englishman. He saw little good in any cultivation of the feelings, and none at all in cultivating them through the imagination, which he thought was only cultivating illusions. It was in vain I urged on him that the imaginative emotion which an idea, when vividly conceived, excites in us, is not an illusion but a fact, as real as any of the other qualities of objects; and, far from implying anything erroneous and delusive in our mental apprehension of the object, is quite consistent with the most accurate knowledge and most perfect practical recognition of all its physical and intellectual laws and relations. The intensest feeling of the beauty of a cloud lighted by the setting sun is no hindrance to my knowing that the cloud is a vapour of water, subject to all the laws of vapours in a state of suspension; and I am just as likely to allow for, and act on, these physical laws whenever there is occasion to do so, as if I had been incapable of perceiving any distinction between beauty and ugliness.

6. Edmund Gosse: *Father and Son*

Edmund Gosse (1849–1928) was the son of Philip Gosse, the eminent nineteenth-century zoologist and Plymouth Brother. He was responsible for introducing Ibsen to the English public and for reviving interest in John Donne, Sir Thomas Browne and Henry Fielding. His gifts were probably dissipated in later years by a growing concern to be part of London's fashionable social life.

Edmund Gosse offers his *Father and Son* to the reader 'as a *document*, as a record of educational and religious conditions which have passed away and will never return'. At this level it is an examination of dying Puritanism. But there is another level which is more personal, for as Gosse says, it is also 'a study of the development of moral and educational ideas during the progress of infancy'. More specifically, the autobiography reveals a dramatic clash between the innate identity of a growing child and a well-meaning but essentially unsympathetic environment.

Out of the darkness of my infancy there comes only one flash of memory. I am seated alone, in my baby-chair, at a dinner-table set for several people. Somebody brings in a leg of mutton, puts it down close to me, and goes out. I am again alone, gazing at two low windows, wide open upon a garden. Suddenly, noiselessly, a large, long animal (obviously a greyhound) appears at one window-sill, slips into the room, seizes the leg of mutton and slips out again. When this happened I could not yet talk. The accomplishment of speech came to me very late, doubtless because I never heard young voices. Many years later, when I mentioned this recollection, there was a shout of laughter and surprise: 'That, then, was what became of the mutton! It was not you, who, as your Uncle A. pretended, ate it up, in the twinkling of an eye, bone and all!'

I suppose that it was the startling intensity of this incident which stamped it upon a memory from which all other impressions of this early date have vanished.

The adventure of the leg of mutton occurred, evidently, at the house of my Mother's brothers, for my parents, at this date, visited no other. My uncles were not religious men, but they had an almost filial respect for my Mother, who was several years senior to the elder of them. When the catastrophe of my grandfather's fortune had occurred, they had not yet left school. My Mother, in spite of an extreme dislike of teaching, which was native to her, immediately accepted the situation of a governess in the family of an Irish nobleman. The mansion was only to be approached, as Miss Edgeworth would have said, 'through eighteen sloughs, at the imminent peril of one's life', and when one had reached it, the mixture of opulence and squalor, of civility and savagery, was unspeakable. But my Mother was well paid, and she stayed in this distasteful environment, doing the work she hated most, while with the margin of her salary she helped first one of her brothers and then the other through his Cambridge course. They studied hard and did well at the university. At length their sister received, in her 'ultima Thule', news that her younger brother had taken his degree, and then and there, with a sigh of intense relief, she resigned her situation and came straight back to England.

It is not to be wondered at, then, that my uncles looked up to their sister with feelings of especial devotion. They were not inclined, they were hardly in a position, to criticize her modes of thought. They were easy-going, cultured and kindly gentlemen, rather limited in their views, without a trace of their sister's force of intellect or her strenuous temper. E. resembled her in person, he was tall, fair, with auburn curls; he cultivated a certain tendency to the Byronic type, fatal and melancholy. A. was short, brown and jocose, with a pretension to common sense; bluff and chatty. As a little child, I adored my Uncle E., who sat silent by the fireside holding me against his knee, saying nothing, but looking unutterably sad, and occasionally shaking his warm-coloured tresses. With great injustice, on the other hand, I detested my Uncle A., because he used to joke in a manner very displeasing to me, and because he would so far forget himself as to chase, and even, if it will be credited, to tickle me. My uncles, who remained bachelors to the end of their lives, earned a comfortable living, E. by teaching, A. as 'something in the City', and they rented an old rambling house in Clapton, that same in which I saw the greyhound. Their house had a strange, delicious smell, so unlike anything I smelt anywhere else, that it used to fill my eyes with tears of mysterious pleasure. I know now that this was the odour of cigars, tobacco being a species of incense tabooed at home on the highest religious grounds.

It has been recorded that I was slow in learning to speak. I used to be told that having met all invitations to repeat such words as 'Papa' and 'Mamma' with gravity and indifference, I one day drew towards me a volume, and said 'book' with startling distinctness. I was not at all precocious, but at a rather early age, I think towards the beginning of my fourth year, I learned to read. I cannot recollect a time when a printed page of English was closed to me. But perhaps earlier still my Mother used to repeat to me a poem which I have always taken for granted that she had herself composed, a poem which had a romantic place in my early mental history. It ran thus, I think:

> O pretty Moon, you shine so bright!
> I'll go to bid Mamma good-night,
> And then I'll lie upon my bed
> And watch you move above my head.
>
> Ah! there, a cloud has hidden you!
> But I can see your light shine thro';
> It tries to hide you – quite in vain,
> For – there you quickly come again!
>
> It's God, I know, that makes you shine
> Upon this little bed of mine;
> But I shall all about you know
> When I can read and older grow.

Long, long after the last line had become an anachronism, I used to shout this poem from my bed before I went to sleep, whether the night happened to be moon-lit or no.

It must have been my Father who taught me my letters. To my Mother, as I have said, it was distasteful to teach, though she was so prompt and skilful to learn. My Father, on the contrary, taught cheerfully, by fits and starts. In particular, he had a scheme for rationalizing geography, which I think was admirable. I was to climb upon a chair, while, standing at my side, with a pencil and a sheet of paper, he was to draw a chart of the markings on the carpet. Then, when I understood the system, another chart on a smaller scale of the furniture in the room, then of a floor of the house, then of the back-garden, then of a section of the street. The result of this was that geography came to me of itself, as a perfectly natural miniature arrangement of objects, and to this day has always been the science which gives me least difficulty. My father also taught me the simple rules of arithmetic, a little natural history, and the elements of drawing; and he laboured long and unsuccessfully to make me learn by heart hymns, psalms and chapters of Scripture, in which I always failed ignominiously and with tears. This puzzled and vexed him, for he himself had an extremely retentive textual memory. He could not help thinking that I was naughty, and would not learn the chapters, until at last he gave up the effort. All this sketch of an education began, I believe, in my fourth year, and was not advanced or modified during the rest of my Mother's life.

Meanwhile, capable as I was of reading, I found my greatest pleasure in the pages of books. The range of these was limited, for story-books of every description were sternly excluded. No fiction of any kind, religious or secular, was admitted into the house. In this it was to my Mother, not to my Father, that the prohibition was due. She had a remarkable, I confess to me still somewhat unaccountable impression that to 'tell a story', that is, to compose fictitious narrative of any kind, was a sin. She carried this conviction to extreme lengths. My Father, in later years, gave me some interesting examples of her firmness. As a young man in America, he had been deeply impressed by 'Salathiel', a pious prose romance by that then popular writer, the Rev. George Croly. When he first met my Mother, he recommended it to her, but she would not consent to open it. Nor would she read the chivalrous tales in verse of Sir Walter Scott, obstinately alleging that they were not 'true'. She would read none but lyrical and subjective poetry. Her secret diary reveals the history of this singular aversion to the fictitious, although it cannot be said to explain the cause of it. As a child, however, she had possessed a passion for making up stories, and so considerable a skill in it that she was constantly being begged to indulge others with its exercise. But I will, on so curious a point, leave her to speak for herself:

When I was a very little child, I used to amuse myself and my brothers with inventing stories, such as I read. Having, as I suppose, naturally a restless mind and busy imagination, this soon became the chief pleasure of my life. Unfortunately, my brothers were always fond of encouraging this propensity, and I found in Taylor, my maid, a still greater tempter. I had not known there was any harm in it, until Miss Shore [a Calvinist governess], finding it out, lectured me severely, and told me it was wicked. From that time forth I considered that to invent a story of any kind was a sin. But the desire to do so was too deeply rooted in my affections to be resisted in my own strength [she was at that time nine years of age], and unfortunately I knew neither my corruption nor my weakness, nor did I know where to gain strength. The longing to invent stories grew with violence; everything I heard or read became food for my distemper. The simplicity of truth was not sufficient for me; I must needs embroider imagination upon it, and the folly, vanity and wickedness which disgraced my heart are more than I am able to express. Even now [at the age of twenty-nine], tho' watched, prayed and striven against, this is still the sin that most easily besets me. It has hindered my prayers and prevented my improvement, and therefore has humbled me very much.

This is, surely, a very painful instance of the repression of an instinct. There seems to have been, in this case, a vocation such as is rarely heard, and still less often wilfully disregarded and silenced. Was my Mother intended by nature to be a novelist? I have often thought so, and her talents and vigour of purpose, directed along the line which was ready to form 'the chief pleasure of her life', could hardly have failed to conduct her to great success. She was a little younger than Bulwer Lytton, a little older than Mrs Gaskell – but these are vain and trivial speculations!

My own state, however, was, I should think, almost unique among the children of cultivated parents. In consequence of the stern ordinance which I have described, not a single fiction was read or told to me during my infancy. The rapture of the child who delays the process of going to bed by cajoling 'a story' out of his mother or his nurse, as he sits upon her knee, well tucked up, at the corner of the nursery fire – this was unknown to me. Never in all my early childhood, did anyone address to me the affecting preamble, 'Once upon a time!' I was told about missionaries, but never about pirates; I was familiar with humming-birds, but I had never heard of fairies. Jack the Giant-Killer, Rumpelstiltskin and Robin Hood were not of my acquaintance, and though I understood about wolves, Little Red Ridinghood was a stranger even by name. So far as my 'dedication' was concerned, I can but think that my parents were in error thus to exclude the imaginary from my outlook upon facts. They desired to make me truthful; the tendency was to make me positive and sceptical. Had they wrapped me in the soft folds of supernatural fancy, my mind might have been longer content to follow their traditions in an unquestioning spirit.

Having easily said what, in those early years, I did not read, I have great difficulty in saying what I did read. But a queer variety of natural history, some of it quite indigestible by my undeveloped mind; many books of travels, mainly of a scientific character, among them voyages of discovery in the South Seas, by which my brain was dimly filled with splendour; some geography and astronomy, both of them sincerely enjoyed; much theology, which I desired to appreciate but could never get my teeth into (if I may venture to say so), and over which my eye and tongue learned to slip without penetrating, so that I would read, and read aloud, and with great propriety of emphasis, page after page without having formed an idea or retained an expression. There was, for instance, a writer on prophecy called Jukes, of whose works each of my parents was inordinately fond, and I was early set to read Jukes aloud to them. I did it glibly, like a machine, but the sight of Jukes' volumes became an abomination to me, and I never formed the outline of a notion what they were about. Later on, a publication called *The Penny Cyclopaedia* became my daily, and for a long time almost my sole study; to the subject of this remarkable work I may presently return.

It is difficult to keep anything like chronological order in recording fragments of early recollection, and in speaking of my reading I have been led too far ahead. My memory does not, practically, begin till we returned from certain visits, made with a zoological purpose, to the shores of Devon and Dorset, and settled, early in my fifth year, in a house at Islington, in the north of London. Our circumstances were now more easy; my Father had regular and well-paid literary work; and the house was larger and more comfortable than ever before, though still very simple and restricted. My memories, some of which are exactly dated by certain facts, now become clear and almost abundant. What I do not remember, except from having it very often repeated to me, is what may be considered the only 'clever' thing that I said during an otherwise unillustrious childhood. It was not startlingly 'clever', but it may pass. A lady – when I was just four – rather injudiciously showed me a large print of a human skeleton, saying, 'There! you don't know what that is, do you?' Upon which, immediately and very archly, I replied, 'Isn't it a man with the meat off?' This was thought wonderful, and, as it is supposed that I had never had the phenomenon explained to me, it certainly displays some quickness in seizing an analogy. I had often watched my Father, while he soaked the flesh off the bones of fishes and small mammals. If I venture to repeat this trifle, it is only to point out that the system on which I was being educated deprived all things, human life among the rest, of their mystery. The 'bare-grinning skeleton of death' was to me merely a prepared specimen of that featherless plantigrade vertebrate, 'homo sapiens'.

As I have said that this anecdote was thought worth repeating, I ought to proceed to say that there was, so far as I can recollect, none of that flattery of childhood which is so often merely a backhanded way of indulging the vanity of parents. My Mother, indeed, would hardly have been human if she had not occasionally entertained herself with the delusion that her solitary duckling was a cygnet. This my Father did not encourage, remarking, with great affection, and chucking me under the chin, that I was 'a nice little ordinary boy'. My Mother, stung by this want of appreciation, would proceed so far as to declare that she believed that in future times the F.R.S. would be chiefly known as his son's father! (This is a pleasantry frequent in professional families.)

To this my Father, whether convinced or not, would make no demur, and the couple would begin to discuss, in my presence, the direction which my shining talents would take. In consequence of my dedication to 'the Lord's Service', the range of possibilities was much restricted. My Father, who had lived long in the Tropics, and who nursed a perpetual nostalgia for 'the little lazy isles where the trumpet-orchids blow', leaned towards the field of missionary labour. My Mother, who was cold about foreign missions, preferred to believe that I should be the Charles Wesley of my age, 'or perhaps', she had the candour to admit, 'merely the George Whitefield'. I cannot recollect the time when I did not understand that I was going to be a minister of the Gospel.

It is so generally taken for granted that a life strictly dedicated to religion is stiff and dreary, that I may have some difficulty in persuading my readers that, as a matter of fact, in these early days of my childhood, before disease and death had penetrated to our slender society, we were always cheerful and often gay. My parents were playful with one another, and there were certain stock family jests which seldom failed to enliven the breakfast table. My Father and Mother lived so completely in the atmosphere of faith, and were so utterly convinced of their intercourse with God, that, so long as that intercourse was not clouded by sin, to which they were delicately sensitive, they could afford to take the passing hour very lightly. They would even, to a certain extent, treat the surroundings of their religion as a subject of jest, joking very mildly and gently about such things as an attitude at prayer or the nature of a supplication. They were absolutely indifferent to forms. They prayed, seated in their chairs, as willingly as, reversed, upon their knees; no ritual having any significance for them. My Mother was sometimes extremely gay, laughing with a soft, merry sound. What I have since been told of the guileless mirth of nuns in a convent has reminded me of the gaiety of my parents during my early childhood.

So long as I was a mere part of them, without individual existence, and swept on, a satellite, in their atmosphere, I was mirthful when they were mirthful, and grave when they were grave. The mere fact that I had no young companions, no story books, no outdoor amusements, none of the thousand and one employments provided for other children in more conventional surroundings, did not make me discontented or fretful, because I did not know of the existence of such entertainments. In exchange, I became keenly attentive to the limited circle of interests open to me. Oddly enough, I have no recollection of any curiosity about other children, nor of any desire to speak to them or play with them. They did not enter into my dreams, which were occupied entirely with grown-up people and animals. I had three dolls, to whom my attitude was not very intelligible. Two of these were female, one with a shapeless face of rags, the other in wax. But, in my fifth year, when the Crimean War broke out, I was given a third doll, a soldier, dressed very smartly in a scarlet cloth tunic. I used to put the dolls on three chairs, and harangue them aloud, but my sentiment to them was never confidential, until our maid-servant one day, intruding on my audience, and misunderstanding the occasion of it, said: 'What? a boy, and playing with a soldier when he's got two lady-dolls to play with?' I had never thought of my dolls as confidants before, but from that time forth I paid a special attention to the soldier, in order to make up to him for Lizzie's unwarrantable insult.

The declaration of war with Russia brought the first breath of outside life into our Calvinist cloister. My parents took in a daily newspaper, which they had never done before, and events in picturesque places, which my Father and I looked out on the map, were eagerly discussed. One of my vividest early memories can be dated exactly. I was playing about the house, and suddenly burst into the breakfast-room, where, close to the door, sat an amazing figure, a very tall young man, as stiff as my doll, in a gorgeous scarlet tunic. Quite far away from him, at her writing-table, my Mother sat with her Bible open before her, and was urging the gospel plan of salvation on his acceptance. She promptly told me to run away and play, but I had seen a great sight. This guardsman was in the act of leaving for the Crimea, and his adventures, – he was converted in consequence of my Mother's instruction, – were afterwards told by her in a tract, called 'The Guardsman of the Alma', of which I believe that more than half a million copies were circulated. He was killed in that battle, and this added an extraordinary lustre to my dream of him. I see him still in my mind's eye, large, stiff, and unspeakably brilliant, seated, from respect, as near as possible to our parlour door. This apparition gave reality to my subsequent conversations with the soldier doll.

That same victory of the Alma, which was reported in London on my fifth birthday, is also marked very clearly in my memory by a family circumstance. We were seated at breakfast, at our small round table drawn close up to the window, my Father with his back to the light. Suddenly, he gave a sort of cry, and read out the opening sentences from *The Times* announcing a battle in the valley of the Alma. No doubt the strain of national anxiety had been very great, for both he and my Mother seemed deeply excited. He broke off his reading when the fact of the decisive victory was assured, and he and my Mother sank simultaneously on their knees in front of their tea and bread-and-butter, while in a loud voice my Father gave thanks to the God of Battles. This patriotism was the more remarkable, in that he had schooled himself, as he believed, to put his 'heavenly citizenship' above all earthly duties. To those who said: 'Because you are a Christian, surely you are not less an Englishman?' he would reply by shaking his head, and by saying: 'I am a citizen of no earthly State'. He did not realize that, in reality, and to use a cant phrase not yet coined in 1854, there existed in Great Britain no more thorough 'Jingo' than he.

Another instance of the remarkable way in which the interests of daily life were mingled, in our strange household, with the practice of religion, made an impression upon my memory. We had all three been much excited by a report that a certain dark geometer-moth, generated in underground stables, had been met with in Islington. Its name, I think, is 'Boletobia fuliginaria', and I believe that it is excessively rare in England. We were sitting at family prayers, on a summer morning, I think in 1855, when through the open window a brown moth came sailing. My Mother immediately interrupted the reading of the Bible by saying to my Father, 'O! Henry, do you think that can be "Boletobia"?' My Father rose up from the sacred book, examined the insect, which had now perched, and replied: 'No! it is only the common Vapourer, "Orgyia antiqua"!', resuming his seat, and the exposition of the Word, without any apology or embarrassment.

In the course of this, my sixth year, there happened a series of minute and soundless incidents which, elementary as they may seem when told, were second in real importance to none in my mental history. The recollection of them confirms me in the opinion that certain leading features in each human soul are inherent to it, and cannot be accounted for by suggestion or training. In my own case, I was most carefully withdrawn, like Princess Blanchefleur in her marble fortress, from every outside influence whatever, yet to me the instinctive life came as unexpectedly as her lover came to her in the basket of roses. What came to me was the consciousness of self, as a force and as a companion, and it came as the result of one or two shocks, which I will relate.

In consequence of hearing so much about an Omniscient God, a being of supernatural wisdom and penetration who was always with us, who made, in fact, a fourth in our company, I had come to think of Him, not without awe, but with absolute confidence.

My Father and Mother, in their serene discipline of me, never argued with one another, never even differed; their wills seemed absolutely one. My Mother always deferred to my Father, and in his absence spoke of him to me, as if he were all-wise. I confused him in some sense with God; at all events I believed that my Father knew everything and saw everything. One morning in my sixth year, my Mother and I were alone in the morning-room, when my Father came in and announced some fact to us. I was standing on the rug, gazing at him, and when he made this statement, I remember turning quickly, in embarrassment, and looking into the fire. The shock to me was as that of a thunderbolt, for what my Father had said 'was not true'. My Mother and I, who had been present at the trifling incident, were aware that it had not happened exactly as it had been reported to him. My Mother gently told him so, and he accepted the correction. Nothing could possibly have been more trifling to my parents, but to me it meant an epoch. Here was the appalling discovery, never suspected before, that my Father was not as God, and did not know everything. The shock was not caused by any suspicion that he was not telling the truth, as it appeared to him, but by the awful proof that he was not, as I had supposed, omniscient.

This experience was followed by another, which confirmed the first, but carried me a great deal further. In our little back-garden, my Father had built up a rockery for ferns and mosses and from the water-supply of the house he had drawn a leaden pipe so that it pierced upwards through the rockery and produced, when a tap was turned, a pretty silvery parasol of water. The pipe was exposed somewhere near the foot of the rockery. One day, two workmen, who were doing some repairs, left their tools during the dinner-hour in the back-garden, and as I was marching about I suddenly thought that to see whether one of these tools could make a hole in the pipe would be attractive. It did make such a hole, quite easily, and then the matter escaped my mind. But a day or two afterwards, when my Father came in to dinner, he was very angry. He had turned the tap, and instead of the fountain arching at the summit, there had been a rush of water through a hole at the foot. The rockery was absolutely ruined.

Of course I realized in a moment what I had done, and I sat frozen with alarm, waiting to be denounced. But my Mother remarked on the visit of the plumbers two or three days before, and my Father instantly took up the suggestion. No doubt that was it; the mischievous fellows had thought it amusing to stab the pipe and spoil the fountain. No suspicion fell on me; no question was asked of me. I sat there, turned to stone within, but outwardly sympathetic and with unchecked appetite.

We attribute, I believe, too many moral ideas to little children. It is obvious that in this tremendous juncture I ought to have been urged forward by good instincts, or held back by naughty ones. But I am sure that the fear which I experienced for a short time, and which so unexpectedly melted away, was a purely physical one. It had nothing to do with the motions of a contrite heart. As to the destruction of the fountain, I was sorry about that, for my own sake, since I admired the skipping water extremely and had had no idea that I was spoiling its display. But the emotions which now thronged within me, and which led me, with an almost unwise alacrity, to seek solitude in the back-garden, were not moral at all, they were intellectual. I was not ashamed of having successfully – and so surprisingly – deceived my parents by my crafty silence; I looked upon that as a providential escape, and dismissed all further thought of it. I had other things to think of.

In the first place, the theory that my Father was omniscient or infallible was now dead and buried. He probably knew very little; in this case he had not known a fact of such importance that if you did not know that, it could hardly matter what you knew. My Father, as a deity, as a natural force of immense prestige, fell in my eyes to a human level. In future, his statements about things in general need not be accepted implicitly. But of all the thoughts which rushed upon my savage and undeveloped little brain at this crisis, the most curious was that I had found a companion and a confidant in myself. There was a secret in this world and it belonged to me and to a somebody who lived in the same body with me. There were two of us, and we could talk with one another. It is difficult to define impressions so rudimentary, but it is certain that it was in this dual form that the sense of my individuality now suddenly descended upon me, and it is equally certain that it was a great solace to me to find a sympathizer in my own breast.

About this time, my Mother, carried away by the current of her literary and her philanthropic work, left me more and more to my own devices. She was seized with a great enthusiasm; as one of her admirers and disciples has written, 'she went on her way, sowing beside all waters'. I would not for a moment let it be supposed that I regard her as a Mrs Jellyby, or that I think she neglected me. But a remarkable work had opened up before her; after her long years in a mental hermitage, she was drawn forth into the clamorous harvest-field of souls. She developed an unexpected gift of persuasion over strangers whom she met in the omnibus or in the train, and with whom she courageously grappled. This began by her noting, with deep humility and joy, that 'I have reason to judge the sound conversion to God of three young persons within a few weeks, by the instrumentality of my conversations with them'. At the same time, as another of her biographers has said, 'those testimonies to the Blood of Christ, the fruits of her pen, began to be spread very widely, even to the most distant parts of the globe'. My Father, too, was at this time at the height of his activity. After breakfast, each of them was amply occupied, perhaps until night-fall; our evenings we still always spent together. Sometimes my Mother took me with her on her 'unknown day's employ'; I recollect pleasant rambles through the City by her side, and the act of looking up at her figure soaring above me. But when all was done, I had hours and hours of complete solitude, in my Father's study, in the back-garden, above all in the garret.

The garret was a fairy place. It was a low lean-to, lighted from the roof. It was wholly unfurnished, except for two objects, an ancient hat-box and a still more ancient skin-trunk. The hat-box puzzled me extremely, till one day, asking my Father what it was, I got a distracted answer which led me to believe that it was itself a sort of hat, and I made a laborious but repeated effort to wear it. The skin-trunk was absolutely empty, but the inside of the lid of it was lined with sheets of what I now know to have been a sensational novel. It was, of course, a fragment, but I read it, kneeling on the bare floor, with indescribable rapture. It will be recollected that the idea of fiction, of a deliberately invented story, had been kept from me with entire success. I therefore implicitly believed the tale in the lid of the trunk to be a true account of the sorrows of a lady of title, who had to flee the country, and who was pursued into foreign lands by enemies bent upon her ruin. Somebody had an interview with a 'minion' in a 'mask'; I went downstairs and looked up these words in Bailey's *English Dictionary*, but was left in darkness as to what they had to do with the lady of title. This ridiculous fragment filled me with delicious fears; I fancied that my Mother, who was out so much, might be threatened by dangers of the same sort; and the fact that the narrative came abruptly to an end, in the middle of one of its most thrilling sentences, wound me up almost to a disorder of wonder and romance.

The preoccupation of my parents threw me more and more upon my own resources. But what are the resources of a solitary child of six? I was never inclined to make friends with servants, nor did our successive maids proffer, so far as I recollect, any advances. Perhaps, with my 'dedication' and my grown-up ways of talking, I did not seem to them at all an attractive little boy. I continued to have no companions, or even acquaintances of my own age. I am unable to recollect exchanging two words with another child till after my Mother's death.

The abundant energy which my Mother now threw into her public work did not affect the quietude of our private life. We had some visitors in the day-time, people who came to consult one parent or the other. But they never stayed to a meal, and we never returned their visits. I do not quite know how it was that neither of my parents took me to any of the sights of London, although I am sure it was a question of principle with them. Notwithstanding all our study of natural history, I was never introduced to live wild beasts at the Zoo, nor to dead ones at the British Museum. I can understand better why we never visited a picture-gallery or a concert-room. So far as I can recollect, the only time I was ever taken to any place of entertainment was when my Father and I paid a visit, long anticipated, to the Great Globe in Leicester Square. This was a huge structure, the interior of which one ascended by means of a spiral staircase. It was a poor affair; that was concave in it which should have been convex, and my imagination was deeply affronted. I could invent a far better Great Globe than that in my mind's eye in the garret.

Being so restricted, then, and yet so active, my mind took refuge in an infantile species of natural magic. This contended with the definite ideas of religion which my parents were continuing, with too mechanical a persistency, to force into my nature, and it ran parallel with them. I formed strange superstitions, which I can only render intelligible by naming some concrete examples. I persuaded myself that, if I could only discover the proper words to say or the proper passes to make, I could induce the gorgeous birds and butterflies in my Father's illustrated manuals to come to life, and fly out of the book, leaving holes behind them. I believed that, when, at the Chapel, we sang, drearily and slowly, loud hymns of experience and humiliation, I could boom forth with a sound equal to that of dozens of singers, if I could only hit upon the formula. During morning and evening prayers, which were extremely lengthy and fatiguing, I fancied that one of my two selves could flit up, and sit clinging to the cornice, and look down on my other self and the rest of us, if I could only find the key. I laboured for hours in search of these formulas, thinking to compass my ends by means absolutely irrational. For example, I was convinced that if I could only count consecutive numbers long enough, without losing one, I should suddenly, on reaching some far-distant figure, find myself in possession of the great secret. I feel quite sure that nothing external suggested these ideas of magic, and I think it probable that they approached the ideas of savages at a very early stage of development.

All this ferment of mind was entirely unobserved by my parents. But when I formed the belief that it was necessary, for the success of my practical magic, that I should hurt myself, and when, as a matter of fact, I began, in extreme secrecy, to run pins into my flesh and bang my joints with books, no one will be surprised to hear that my Mother's attention was drawn to the fact that I was looking 'delicate'. The notice nowadays universally given to the hygienic rules of life was rare fifty years ago and among deeply religious people, in particular, fatalistic views of disease prevailed. If any one was ill, it showed that 'the Lord's hand was extended in chastisement', and much prayer was poured forth in order that it might be explained to the sufferer, or to his relations, in what he or they had sinned. People would, for instance, go on living over a cess-pool, working themselves up into an agony to discover how they had incurred the displeasure of the Lord, but never moving away. As I became very pale and nervous, and slept badly at nights, with visions and loud screams in my sleep, I was taken to a physician who, stripped me and tapped me all over (this gave me some valuable hints for my magical practices), but could find nothing the matter. He recommended, – whatever physicians in such cases always recommend, – but nothing was done. If I was feeble it was the Lord's Will, and we must acquiesce.

It culminated in a sort of fit of hysterics, when I lost all self-control, and sobbed with tears, and banged my head on the table. While this was proceeding, I was conscious of that dual individuality of which I have already spoken, since while one part of me gave way, and could not resist, the other part in some extraordinary sense seemed standing aloof, much impressed. I was alone with my Father when this crisis suddenly occurred, and I was interested to see that he was greatly alarmed. It was a very long time since we had spent a day out of London, and I said, on being coaxed back to calmness, that I wanted 'to go into the country'. Like the dying Falstaff, I babbled of green fields. My Father, after a little reflection, proposed to take me to Primrose Hill. I had never heard of the place, and names have always appealed directly to my imagination. I was in the highest degree delighted, and could hardly restrain my impatience. As soon as possible we set forth westward, my hand in my Father's, with the liveliest anticipations. I expected to see a mountain absolutely carpeted with primroses, a terrestrial galaxy like that which covered the hill that led up to Montgomery Castle in Donne's poem. But at length, as we walked from the Chalk Farm direction, a miserable acclivity stole into view – surrounded, even in those days, on most sides by houses, with its grass worn to the buff by millions of boots, and resembling what I meant by 'the country' about as much as Poplar resembles Paradise. We sat down on a bench at its inglorious summit, whereupon I burst into tears, and in a heart-rending whisper sobbed, 'Oh! Papa, let us go home!'

This was the lachrymose epoch in a career not otherwise given to weeping, for I must tell one more tale of tears. About this time, – the autumn of 1855, – my parents were disturbed more than once in the twilight, after I had been put to bed, by shrieks from my crib. They would rush up to my side, and find me in great distress, but would be unable to discover the cause of it. The fact was that I was half beside myself with ghostly fears, increased and pointed by the fact that there had been some daring burglaries in our street. Our servant-maid, who slept at the top of the house, had seen, or thought she saw, upon a moonlight night, the figure of a crouching man, silhouetted against the sky, slip down from the roof and leap into her room. She screamed, and he fled away. Moreover, as if this were not enough for my tender nerves, there had been committed a horrid murder, at a baker's shop just round the corner in the Caledonian Road, to which murder actuality was given to us by the fact that my Mother had been 'just thinking' of getting her bread from this shop. Children, I think, were not spared the details of these affairs fifty years ago; at least, I was not, and my nerves were a packet of spilikins.

But what made me scream o' nights was that when my Mother had tucked me up in bed and had heard me say my prayer, and had prayed aloud on her knees at my side, and had stolen downstairs, noises immediately began in the room. There was a rustling of clothes, and a slapping of hands, and a gurgling, and a sniffing, and a trotting. These horrible muffled sounds would go on, and die away, and be resumed; I would pray very fervently to God to save me from my enemies; and sometimes I would go to sleep. But on other occasions, my faith and fortitude alike gave way, and I screamed 'Mama! Mama!' Then would my parents come bounding up the stairs, and comfort me, and kiss me, and assure me it was nothing. And nothing it was while they were there, but no sooner had they gone than the ghostly riot recommenced. It was at last discovered by my Mother that the whole mischief was due to a card of framed texts, fastened by one nail to the wall; this did nothing when the bedroom door was shut, but when it was left open (in order that my parents might hear me call), the card began to gallop in the draught, and made the most intolerable noises.

Several things tended at this time to alienate my conscience from the line which my Father had so rigidly traced for it. The question of the efficacy of prayer, which has puzzled wiser heads than mine was, began to trouble me. It was insisted on in our household that if anything was desired, you should not, as my Mother said, 'lose any time in seeking for it, but ask God to guide you to it'. In many junctures of life this is precisely what, in sober fact, they did. I will not dwell here on their theories, which my Mother put forth, with unflinching directness, in her published writings. But I found that a difference was made between my privileges in this matter and theirs, and this led to many discussions. My parents said: 'Whatever you need, tell Him and He will grant it, if it is His will.' Very well; I had need of a large painted humming-top which I had seen in a shop-window in the Caledonian Road. Accordingly, I introduced a supplication for this object into my evening prayer, carefully adding the words: 'If it is Thy will.' This, I recollect, placed my Mother in a dilemma, and she consulted my Father. Taken, I suppose, at a disadvantage, my Father told me I must not pray for 'things like that'. To which I answered by another query, 'Why?' And I added that he said we ought to pray for things we needed, and that I needed the humming-top a great deal more than I did the conversion of the heathen or the restitution of Jerusalem to the Jews, two objects of my nightly supplication which left me very cold.

I have reason to believe, looking back upon this scene, conducted by candle-light in the front parlour, that my Mother was much baffled by the logic of my argument. She had gone so far as to say publicly that no 'things or circumstances are too insignificant to bring before the God of the whole earth'. I persisted that this covered the case of the humming-top, which was extremely significant to me. I noticed that she held aloof from the discussion, which was carried on with some show of annoyance by my Father. He had never gone quite so far as she did in regard to this question of praying for material things. I am not sure that she was convinced that I ought to have been checked; but he could not help seeing that it reduced their favourite theory to an absurdity for a small child to exercise the privilege. He ceased to argue, and told me peremptorily that it was not right for me to pray for things like humming-tops, and that I must do it no more. His authority, of course, was paramount, and I yielded; but my faith in the efficacy of prayer was a good deal shaken. The fatal suspicion had crossed my mind that the reason why I was not to pray for the top was because it was too expensive for my parents to buy, that being the usual excuse for not getting things I wished for.

It was about the date of my sixth birthday that I did something very naughty, some act of direct disobedience, for which my Father, after a solemn sermon, chastised me, sacrificially, by giving me several cuts with a cane. This action was justified, as everything he did was justified, by reference to Scripture – 'Spare the rod and spoil the child'. I suppose that there are some children, of a sullen and lymphatic temperament, who are smartened up and made more wide-awake by a whipping. It is largely a matter of convention, the exercise being endured (I am told) with pride by the infants of our aristocracy, but not tolerated by the lower classes. I am afraid that I proved my inherent vulgarity by being made, not contrite or humble, but furiously angry by this caning. I cannot account for the flame of rage which it awakened in my bosom. My dear, excellent Father had beaten me, not very severely, without ill-temper, and with the most genuine desire to improve me. But he was not well-advised especially so far as the 'dedication to the Lord's service' was concerned. This same 'dedication' had ministered to my vanity, and there are some natures which are not improved by being humiliated. I have to confess with shame that I went about the house for some days with a murderous hatred of my Father locked within my bosom. He did not suspect that the chastisement had not been wholly efficacious, and he bore me no malice; so that after a while, I forgot and thus forgave him. But I do not regard physical punishment as a wise element in the education of proud and sensitive children.

My theological misdeeds culminated, however, in an act so puerile and preposterous that I should not venture to record it if it did not throw some glimmering of light on the subject which I have proposed to myself in writing these pages. My mind continued to dwell on the mysterious question of prayer. It puzzled me greatly to know why, if we were God's children, and if he was watching over us by night and day, we might not supplicate for toys and sweets and smart clothes as well as for the conversion of the heathen. Just at this juncture, we had a special service at the Room, at which our attention was particularly called to what we always spoke of as 'the field of missionary labour'. The East was represented among 'the saints' by an excellent Irish peer, who had, in his early youth, converted and married a lady of colour; this Asiatic shared in our Sunday morning meetings, and was an object of helpless terror to me; I shrank from her amiable caresses, and vaguely identified her with a personage much spoken of in our family circle, the 'Personal Devil'.

All these matters drew my thoughts to the subject of idolatry, which was severely censured at the missionary meeting. I cross-examined my Father very closely as to the nature of this sin, and pinned him down to the categorical statement that idolatry consisted in praying to any one or anything but God himself. Wood and stone, in the words of the hymn, were peculiarly liable to be bowed down to by the heathen in their blindness. I pressed my Father further on this subject, and he assured me that God would be very angry, and would signify His anger, if anyone, in a Christian country, bowed down to wood and stone. I cannot recall why I was so pertinacious on this subject, but I remember that my Father became a little restive under my cross-examination. I determined, however, to test the matter for myself, and one morning, when both my parents were safely out of the house, I prepared for the great act of heresy. I was in the morning-room on the ground-floor, where, with much labour, I hoisted a small chair on to the table close to the window. My heart was now beating as if it would leap out of my side, but I pursued my experiment. I knelt down on the carpet in front of the table and looking up I said my daily prayer in a loud voice, only substituting the address 'O Chair!' for the habitual one.

Having carried this act of idolatry safely through, I waited to

A.E.—4

see what would happen. It was a fine day, and I gazed up at the slip of white sky above the houses opposite, and I expected something to appear in it. God would certainly exhibit his anger in some terrible form, and would chastise my impious and wilful action. I was very much alarmed, but still more excited; I breathed the high, sharp air of defiance. But nothing happened; there was not a cloud in the sky, not an unusual sound in the street. Presently I was quite sure that nothing would happen. I had committed idolatry, flagrantly and deliberately, and God did not care.

The result of this ridiculous act was not to make me question the existence and power of God; those were forces which I did not dream of ignoring. But what it did was to lessen still further my confidence in my Father's knowledge of the Divine mind. My Father had said, positively, that if I worshipped a thing made of wood, God would manifest his anger. I had then worshipped a chair, made (or partly made) of wood, and God had made no sign whatever. My Father, therefore, was not really acquainted with the Divine practice in cases of idolatry. And with that, dismissing the subject, I dived again into the unplumbed depths of the *Penny Cyclopaedia*.

7. Maxim Gorki:
My Childhood

Maxim Gorki (1868–1936) was born in the city of Nizhny Novgorod. From the age of eight he had to support himself by various menial jobs. He began to write stories about the people he worked with and met, gipsies, fishermen, tramps, factory-workers, and became, in time, a central figure in twentieth-century Russian Literature. In 1905 he was arrested by the Tsarist government for his revolutionary beliefs, and in 1906 he escaped to America. He returned to Moscow in 1928 to spend the last six years of his life there.

My Childhood is the first of a trilogy (the other two volumes are *Among the People* and *My Universities*) describing the first eight years of his life. It begins with the funeral of his father and the return of Maxim and his mother to his grandparents. Much of his experience in these eight years is violent and sordid. At eight, when his mother dies, Maxim is compelled to leave the house and find his own living. Yet the autobiography asserts the imperishable flame of the human spirit.

'Life', writes Maxim Gorki, 'is always surprising us, not by its rich seething layer of bestial refuse – but by the bright, healthy and creative human powers of goodness that are for ever forcing their way up through it. It is these powers that awaken our indestructible hope that a brighter, better and more human life will once again be born.'

Father lay on the floor, by the window of a small, darkened room, dressed in white, and looking terribly long. His feet were bare and his toes were strangely splayed out. His gentle fingers, now peacefully resting on his chest, were also distorted, and the black disks of copper coins firmly sealed his once shining eyes. His kind face had darkened and its nastily bared teeth frightened me.

Mother, half naked in a red skirt, was kneeling beside him, combing his long soft hair down from the forehead to the nape of his neck with the black comb I loved to use as a saw for melon rinds. She kept muttering something in a hoarse, deep voice. Her grey eyes were swollen and seemed to be dissolving in a flood of tears.

Grandmother was holding me by the hand. She was a fat, round woman with a large head, enormous eyes and a funny, puffy nose. All black and soft, she was terribly fascinating. She was crying as well, her voice pitched differently from Mother's but in a way that perfectly harmonized with it. Shaking all over, she pulled and pushed me over to Father. I stubbornly resisted and tried to hide behind her, for I felt frightened and out of place there.

I'd never seen grown-ups crying before and couldn't make head or tail of the words Grandmother repeated again and again:

'Say good-bye to your father. You won't ever see him again, dear. He died too young, before his time. . . .'

I'd been very ill and had only just started walking again. During my illness – and this I remember very clearly – Father had lightheartedly played games with me and kept me amused. And then he suddenly disappeared and a new person, Grandmother, took his place.

'Where did you walk down from?' I asked her.

She answered: 'From up the river, from Nizhny. But I didn't walk – I came by boat! You can't walk on water! Enough of your questions now!'

This I found both funny and puzzling. Upstairs in the house lived two bearded Persians, while the cellar was occupied by an old, sallow-faced Kalmuck who sold sheepskins. I could slide down the banisters or somersault down if I fell off – that was an accepted fact. But what did water have to do with it?

It all seemed wrong and ludicrously mixed up.

'And why should I be quiet?'

'Because you've always too much to say for yourself,' she said, laughing.

The way she spoke was warm, cheerful, rhythmical. We became firm friends from the very first day, and now I wanted both of us to get out of that room as soon as possible.

Mother's presence had a stifling effect on me and her tears and wailing awakened an unfamiliar feeling of anxiety in me. I'd never seen her like that before: she had always been stern with me and was given to few words. She was a clean, smooth, large person, like a horse. She had a firm body and extremely strong hands. And now she looked unpleasantly swollen and dishevelled. All her clothes were torn. Her hair, which was usually neatly combed into place like a large gay hat, was scattered over her bare shoulders, and hung over her face, and some of it, in the form of a large plait, dangled about, touching Father's sleeping face. For all the time I'd been standing in that room, not once did she so much as look at me, but just went on combing Father's hair, choking with tears and howling continually.

Some dark-skinned peasants and a local constable peered round the door. 'Hurry up and get him out of here!' the constable shouted angrily.

A dark shawl had been used as a curtain over the window and it swelled out like a sail. Once Father had taken me sailing and suddenly there was a thunderclap. Father had laughed, pressed me firmly between his knees and shouted: 'It's nothing, don't be frightened, Alex!'

Suddenly Mother lifted herself heavily from the floor, then fell down on her back, so that her hair brushed over the floor. Her unseeing, pale face had gone blue. Baring her teeth like Father's, she said in a terrifying voice: 'Close the door. Get Alexei out of here!'

Grandmother pushed me aside as she made for the door.

'Friends, don't be afraid,' she cried. 'Don't touch her. And go away, for Christ's sake! It's not cholera. She's in labour – please go away!'

I hid in a dim corner behind a trunk and looked from there

at Mother writhing over the floor, groaning and gnashing her teeth, while Grandmother crawled round her and said in a gentle, joyful voice:

'In the name of the Son and the Holy Ghost! Try and bear the pain, Varyusha! Holy Mother of God who prays for us. . . .'

I was frightened out of my wits: there they were rolling over the floor, knocking up against Father's body, groaning and shouting; he didn't move and seemed to be laughing. This went on for a long time, and several times Mother got to her feet only to fall down again.

Grandmother kept rolling in and out of the room like a big black soft ball. Suddenly a baby cried in the darkness.

'God be praised!' said Grandmother. 'A boy!' And she lit a candle.

I must have dozed off in a corner as I don't remember anything more.

Another vivid experience that stands out in my memory is a rainy day in a deserted corner of a cemetery. I stood on a slippery heap of stocky mud and looked down into the pit where my father's coffin had been lowered. At the bottom was a lot of water, and a few frogs. Two of them had succeeded in climbing on to the yellow coffin lid. My grandmother, myself, a policeman who looked soaked to the skin, and two men with spades who were evidently in a very bad mood, had gathered round the grave. A warm rain, as fine as delicate beads, began to fall gently on us.

'Fill it in,' said the policeman as he walked away.

Grandmother burst into tears and hid her face in her shawl. The gravediggers, bent double, began piling the earth into the grave at great speed. Water squelched. The frogs jumped off the coffin and tried to escape up the sides, but were thrown back by clods of earth.

'Let's go now, Lenya,' said Grandmother as she put her hand on my shoulder. Reluctant to leave, I slipped out of her grasp.

'God help us,' she grumbled – not at me, or even at God, and she stood by the grave for a long time, quite silent. Even when the grave had been levelled off she still stood there.

The gravediggers smacked their spades against the mud, which made them ring out with a hollow sound. A sudden gust of wind drove away the rain.

Grandmother took my hand and led me to a distant church surrounded by a great number of dark crosses.

'Why don't you cry?' she asked when we left the cemetery. 'You *ought* to cry.'

'I don't want to,' I replied.

'Well, you'd better not if you don't want to,' she said softly.

I found this very strange. When I did cry, which wasn't often, it was usually because of some insult, and not from physical pain; my father always laughed at me, but Mother would shout:

'Don't you dare cry!'

Afterwards we drove in a droshky along a broad and very muddy street lined with houses painted deep red. I asked Grandmother:

'Will the frogs get out?'

'No, they don't stand a chance, God help them!'

Neither my mother nor my father ever mentioned the name of God so often and with such familiarity.

A few days later we were all travelling in a small cabin on board a steamboat. My newly-born brother Maxim had died and lay on a table in the corner, wrapped up in a white sheet tied round with red ribbon.

I clambered up on to the piles of luggage and trunks, and looked out of the porthole, which was round and bulging like a horse's eye. Beyond the wet glass the swirling foamy water stretched away endlessly. At times it seemed to rear up and lick the glass, making me jump back on to the floor.

'Don't be frightened,' said Grandmother as she gently lifted me in her soft arms and put me back on the pile of luggage.

A grey, damp mist hung over the water. Somewhere, in the distance, a dark mass of land would loom up, and then disappear. Everything around me was shaking. Only my mother, who was leaning against a wall, her hands behind her head, stood firm and steady.

Her face, clouded over, grimly set and with the eyes shut tight, was that of a blind person. Not once did she speak. She seemed to have changed into somebody else, strange and new. Even her dress was different.

Grandmother asked her over and over again, in the soft voice she had:

'Varya dear, try and eat something, won't you?'

My mother didn't reply and remained motionless.

Grandmother used to whisper to me; with my mother she raised her voice, but all the same approached her timidly and cautiously, saying very little. It struck me that she was afraid of her. This I could well understand, and I felt all the closer to my grandmother.

'Saratov!' my mother exclaimed in an unexpectedly loud and angry voice. 'Where's that sailor got to?'

The words 'Saratov' and 'sailor' were very strange and foreign-sounding.

A broad-shouldered, grey-haired man, dressed in blue, came into the cabin. He carried a small box. Grandmother took it from him and began to lay out my brother. When she had finished she took the box in her outstretched arms to the door. But she was far too fat to get through the narrow door-way – except sideways – and her confusion and embarrassment made me laugh.

'Oh, Mother!' my mother cried, and took away the coffin. They both disappeared, leaving me staring at the man in blue.

'What, has your brother gone?' he said, leaning towards me.

'Who are you?'

'A sailor.'

'And who is Saratov?'

'Saratov's a town. Look out of the window . . . there!'

Through the window I could see the land slipping by. It was dark and steep, and the mist rose from it in smoky rings, reminding me of a large slice of bread freshly cut from the loaf.

'And where's Grandmother gone?'

'To bury her grandson.'

'Will they put him in the ground?'

'Of course. How else can they bury him?'

I told the sailor about the frogs buried alive with my father. He lifted me in his arms, gave me a firm hug and kissed me.

'You're too young to understand!' he said. 'You don't have to be sorry for the frogs, to hell with them! It's your mother you should pity. . . . See what life's done to *her*!'

Suddenly something hooted and roared above. I knew very well that it was the ship, and I wasn't at all afraid. But the sailor hurriedly put me down on the floor and rushed off saying:

'I've got to run!'

I wanted to run as well. I went out of the cabin. The dim narrow gangway was empty. Near the door, copper plates glinted on the ladder steps. I looked up and saw people with knapsacks and bundles. Clearly everybody was leaving the ship, and that meant I had to go too.

When I found myself in the middle of a crowd of men by the

rail, just in front of the gangway, everyone started shouting at me:
'Who do you belong to?'
'Don't know.'

For a long time I was shoved around, shaken and poked. At last the grey-haired sailor appeared on the scene and seized me.

'He's the boy from one of the cabins, from Astrakhan,' he explained. He ran with me into the cabin, dumped me on a pile of luggage and pointed a menacing finger at me as he left.

'Don't you dare move!'

The noise up above gradually died down. The ship was steadily throbbing now and no longer pitched and tossed through the water. Something that looked like a wet wall shut out the light at the porthole. The cabin became dark and stuffy and the bundles of luggage seemed to swell up, crowding me out and making me feel cramped and ill at ease. Perhaps I'd been left alone on that empty ship for good?

I went to the door but couldn't budge the copper handle. I caught hold of a bottle of milk and smashed it against the handle as hard as I could. The milk drenched my legs and trickled right down to my shoes.

Angry at this failure, I lay down on the luggage and softly cried, after which I fell asleep with the tears still rolling down my cheeks.

When I woke up, the boat was shaking all over again and pounding through the water. Like the sun, the porthole seemed to be on fire. Grandmother was sitting near me, combing her hair and frowning as she muttered to herself. She had amazingly long hair – black streaked with blue – that reached right down to the floor, falling over her shoulders, breasts and knees. She would lift the long plaits with one hand and force a wooden comb, which only had a few teeth, through them with great difficulty. Her lips twisted and her dark eyes shone angrily, and her face, framed by that huge mass of hair, became small and comical.

Today she seemed in a bad temper, but when I asked her why she had such long hair, she told me in the same soft and warm voice as yesterday:

'It's one of God's ways of punishing me – it's the devil's own job combing the damned stuff out! Ever since I was a little girl I used to boast about my lion's mane. Now it's the curse of my life! Time you were asleep! It's still very early, the sun's only just risen.'

'But I don't want to sleep!'

'Then don't!' she agreed at once, plaiting her hair and looking at the divan where my mother lay, face upwards, taut as a violin string. 'Tell me how you broke that bottle yesterday. But quietly!'

When she spoke she seemed almost to sing her words and this made them take root firmly in my memory, like flowers – soft, bright and full of richness. When she smiled, the pupils of her dark cherry-coloured eyes opened wide blazing with a light that was too welcoming for words, and her strong white teeth were laid bare. In spite of the many wrinkles in the swarthy skin round her cheeks, her whole face suddenly became young and radiant again. What spoiled it was that puffy nose with its inflated nostrils and red tip – she took snuff which she kept in a black box decorated with silver. A dark figure, she shone from within with a warm, cheering light. Although she had a bad stoop and was almost hunchbacked, and fat into the bargain, she moved with a surprising ease and agility, like a large cat – and she was just as soft as that affectionate animal.

Before she came into my life I must have been lying asleep in a dark corner, but now she had woken me up, brought me out into the light, and bound up everything around me into a continuous thread which she wove into many-coloured lace. At once she became a friend for life, nearest to my heart, and the person I treasured and understood more than anyone else. It was her unselfish love of the world that enriched me and nourished me with the strength I would need for the hard life that lay ahead.

Forty years ago steamboats moved slowly. It took us ages to reach Nizhny, and I clearly remember that time when I first experienced nature's beauty to the full.

The weather had set in fair. From morning to night I would walk with Grandmother on the deck, under a cloudless sky, the banks of the Volga on either side looking like woven silk tinted with the gold of autumn. Without any hurry, slowly moving its rumbling paddles through the grey-blue water, a bright red-coloured steamboat swung up the river with a barge in tow, grey – just like a woodlouse. The sun moved up imperceptibly above the Volga. Every moment there was something new to look at, the scene was changing the whole time. The green hills looked like folds in the rich dress of the earth. Towns and villages lined the banks, and from a distance seemed to be made of gingerbread. Golden autumn leaves floated in the water.

'Look how beautiful it is!' Grandmother would exclaim as she went from one side of the boat to the other. Her face shone and her eyes were wide open with joy. She was so engrossed with looking at the bank, I might not have been there at all. She would stand at the rail, her hands folded across her breast. Then she would smile, not saying a word, and with tears in her eyes. I would pull at her dark flower-patterned skirt.

'What?' she would say with a start. 'I must have dozed off. It's all like a dream!'

'Why are you crying?'

'Because I'm so happy, dear – and so old,' she said, smiling. 'I'm an old woman. I've seen more than sixty years – just torn past they have.' After a pinch of snuff she would begin her wonderful stories about good robbers, saints, and all kinds of wild animals and evil spirits.

She would tell these stories in a soft, mysterious voice, her face turned towards me. Her wide-open eyes would stare into mine as if she were pouring strength into my heart, which uplifted me.

She seemed to sing the stories to me, and the longer she went on, the more harmonious and flowing the words became. Listening to her was the most marvellous experience. I would sit there, and then ask her: 'More!'

'It was like this: an old goblin was sitting by the fire when he got a splinter of vermicelli in his hand. He rocked to and fro with pain and whined: "Oh, little mice, I can't stand the pain!" ' She would lift her leg up high, grip it and shake it, comically wrinkling up her face as if she were in pain herself.

Some bearded sailors were standing by us. All of them looked very kind and they applauded and laughed as they listened to Grandmother's stories.

'Now, Grandma, let's have some more,' they kept on asking. Then they said: 'Come and have a bite with us.'

They gave Grandmother vodka and I was treated to watermelons and canteloupes. These had to be eaten secretly, for there was a man on board who forbade anyone to eat fruit and if he found any would take it away and throw it into the river. He was dressed like a policeman, with brass buttons on his uniform, and he was always drunk. Everyone hid when they saw him coming.

My mother rarely went on deck, and never came near us. She said nothing all the time we were on the boat. Her large, shapely body, her dark emotionless face, her heavy crown of bright, plaited hair, her firmness and strength – all this I can picture now as though I were seeing her through a mist or a transparent cloud, from which her grey eyes, large as Grandmother's, peered out coldly and distantly.

Once she said sternly:

'People are always laughing at you, Mamma!'

'Let them!' answered Grandmother in an unconcerned voice. 'Let them laugh. It's good for them!'

I remember Grandmother's childlike joy when she first saw Nizhny. Holding me by the hand, she pulled me to the rail and cried:

'Just look! It's so beautiful! Nizhny! What a city! Can you see those churches there – they seem to be flying through the air!'

She was near to tears as she asked Mother:

'Varyusha, why don't you come and have a look? Just for a moment. Cheer up now!'

Mother produced a gloomy smile.

When the boat dropped anchor opposite the beautiful city, in the middle of a river crowded with boats and bristling with hundreds of pointed masts, a large rowing-boat full of people came alongside and hooked on to the lowered rope ladder. One by one the people climbed up. In front of everyone else was a small, shrivelled-looking old man in long black clothes and with a beard of tarnished gold. He had a nose like a bird's beak, and small green eyes, and he climbed rapidly to the top of the ladder.

'Father!' my mother cried in a loud deep voice and flung herself into his arms. He seized her head, swiftly stroked her cheeks with his small reddish hands and screeched:

'And how's my silly girl, eh? Now, now. You've come at last!'

Grandmother managed to embrace and kiss everyone at once and she spun round like a propeller. She pushed me forwards and said hurriedly:

'Move yourself now. This is Uncle Mikhail, and this is Uncle Yakov . . . Auntie Natalya, and these are your cousins, both called Sasha, and your cousin Katerina . . . it's a big family!'

Grandfather said to her: 'Are you well?' They kissed each other three times.

Grandfather hauled me away from the thick mob and asked me, holding me by the head:

'And who might you be?'

'I'm from Astrakhan, from the cabin. . . .'

'What's he talking about?' Grandfather said to Mother.

Without giving me time to reply, he pushed me to one side and said: 'He's got his father's cheekbones. . . . Get into the boat!'

We reached the shore and we all went up the hill along a road made of large cobbles, high embankments overgrown with rank trampled grass lining it on either side.

Grandfather and Mother led the way. Grandfather only came up to her shoulder and he took small, mincing steps while Mother glanced down at him and seemed to glide through the air. My uncles followed silently: Mikhail with his sleek black hair and the same withered look as Grandfather; and Yakov, his hair bright and curly. Then came some fat women in gay dresses, and six children, all older than me and all very subdued. I walked with Grandmother and my little Aunt Natalya. Pale-faced, blue-eyed, with an enormous belly, she stopped every now and again, and panted for breath: 'I can't go any further,' she complained.

'Why did they have to bring *you* along?' Grandmother mumbled angrily. 'They've got no sense at all!'

I didn't like the grown-ups, nor the children, and I felt completely and utterly lost in their company. Even Grandmother seemed to recede into the background and became a stranger to me. I took a particular dislike to Grandfather, immediately sensing he was an enemy. For this reason I watched him closely, taking care lest my curiosity led me into danger.

We reached the end of the path. At the very top, leaning against the embankment on the right, and the very first house in the street, stood a squat, single-storeyed house painted dirty pink, with a roof hanging low over its bulging windows like a hat pulled down. From the street it looked very big, but inside its dim little rooms it was very cramped. Angry people rushed about in all directions like passengers about to disembark from a ship, ragged children swarmed all over the place like thieving sparrows, and the whole house was filled with a strange pungent smell.

I stood outside in the yard, which was just as unpleasant: all around it hung huge wet rags and it was full of tubs containing oily-looking water, all different colours. Pieces of cloth were being dipped into them. In one corner, under a ramshackle lean-to, wood burnt fiercely in a stove. I could hear water boiling and bubbling and someone I couldn't see was shouting, very loudly, these strange words: 'Sandalwood, magenta, vitriol. . . .'

8. Carl Gustav Jung:
Memories, Dreams, Reflections

Jung (1875–1966) was the son of the Reverend Paul Jung, a Protestant minister. By 1900 he had completed his medical studies and become an assistant at the Mental Hospital at Zurich where he found himself deeply interested in the pathological variants of normality. In 1907 he met Freud and for a time they collaborated, visiting America together in 1909 to lecture at Clark University, Massachusetts. The friendship however was shortlived for Jung refused to accept Freud's insistence on a sexual interpretation of symbolism, claiming it was too exclusive and dogmatic. After his break with Freud, Jung courageously explored his own psyche and in the process began to formulate such concepts as the archetypes, the collective unconscious, psychological types and psychic energy. His own understanding of man's culture and psychology was elaborated in a series of books including *Psychological Types*, *The Development of the Personality*, and *Symbols of Transformation*.

Jung did not begin preparing his autobiography till 1957. It is preoccupied with the inward events of his life. In the Prologue to *Memories, Dreams, Reflections* Jung wrote:

'I early arrived at the insight that when no answer comes from within to the problems and complexities of life, they ultimately mean very little. Outward circumstances are no substitute for inner experience. Therefore my life has been singularly poor in outward happenings. I cannot tell much about them, for it would strike me as hollow and insubstantial. I can understand myself only in the light of inner happenings. It is these that make up the singularity of my life, and with these my autobiography deals.'

School came to bore me. It took up far too much time which I would rather have spent drawing battles and playing with fire. Divinity classes were unspeakably dull, and I felt a downright fear of the mathematics class. The teacher pretended that algebra was a perfectly natural affair, to be taken for granted, whereas I didn't even know what numbers really were. They were not flowers, not animals, not fossils; they were nothing that could be imagined, mere quantities that resulted from counting. To my confusion these quantities were now represented by letters, which signified sounds, so that it became possible to hear them, so to speak. Oddly enough, my classmates could handle these things, and found them self-evident. No one could tell me what numbers were, and I was unable even to formulate the question. To my horror I found that no one understood my difficulty. The teacher, I must admit, went to great lengths to explain to me the purpose of this curious operation of translating understandable quantities into sounds. I finally grasped that what was aimed at was a kind of system of abbreviation, with the help of which many quantities could be put in a short formula. But this did not interest me in the least. I thought the whole business was entirely arbitrary. Why should numbers be expressed by sounds? One might just as well express a by apple tree, b by box and x by a question mark. a, b, c, x, y, z were not concrete and did not explain to me anything about the essence of numbers, any more than an apple tree did. But the thing that exasperated me most of all was the proposition: If $a = b$ and $b = c$, then $a = c$, even though by definition a meant something other than b and, being different, could therefore not be equated with b, let alone with c. Whenever it was a question of an equivalence, then it was said that $a = a$, $b = b$, and so on. This I could accept, whereas $a = b$ seemed to me a downright lie or a fraud. I was equally outraged when the teacher stated in the teeth of his own definition of parallel lines that they met at infinity. This seemed to me no better than a stupid trick to catch peasants with, and I could not and would not have anything to do with it. My intellectual morality fought against these whimsical inconsistencies, which have forever debarred me from understanding mathematics. Right into old age I have had the incorrigible feeling that if, like my schoolmates, I could have accepted without a struggle the proposition that $a = b$, or that sun = moon, dog = cat, then mathematics might have fooled me endlessly – just *how* much I only began to realize at the age of eighty-four. All my life it remained a puzzle to me why it was that I never managed to get my bearings in mathematics when there was no doubt whatever that I could calculate properly. Least of all did I understand my own *moral* doubts concerning mathematics.

Equations I could comprehend only by inserting specific numerical values in place of the letters and verifying the meaning of the operation by actual calculation. As we went on in mathematics I was able to get along, more or less, by copying out algebraic formulas whose meaning I did not understand, and by memorizing where a particular combination of letters had stood on the blackboard. I could no longer make headway by substi-

tuting numbers, for from time to time the teacher would say,
'Here we put the expression so-and-so,' and then he would
scribble a few letters on the blackboard. I had no idea where he
got them and why he did it – the only reason I could see was that
it enabled him to bring the procedure to what he felt was a
satisfactory conclusion. I was so intimidated by my incomprehen-
sion that I did not dare to ask any questions.

Mathematics classes became sheer terror and torture to me.
Other subjects I found easy; and, as, thanks to my good visual
memory, I contrived for a long while to swindle my way through
mathematics, I usually had good marks. But my fear of failure and
my sense of smallness in face of the vast world around me created
in me not only a dislike but a kind of silent despair which completely ruined school for me. In addition I was exempted from
drawing classes on grounds of utter incapacity. This in a way was
welcome to me, since it gave me more free time; but on the other
hand it was a fresh defeat, since I had some facility in drawing,
although I did not realize that it depended essentially on the way
I was feeling. I could draw only what stirred my imagination.
But I was forced to copy prints of Greek gods with sightless eyes,
and when that wouldn't go properly the teacher obviously
thought I needed something more naturalistic and set before me
the picture of a goat's head. The assignment I failed completely
and that was the end of my drawing-classes.

To my defeats in mathematics and drawing there was now
added a third: from the very first I hated gymnastics. I could not
endure having others tell me how to move. I was going to school
in order to learn something, not to practise useless and senseless
acrobatics. Moreover, as a result of my earlier accidents, I had a
certain physical timidity which I was not able to overcome until
much later on. This timidity was in turn linked with a distrust of
the world and its potentialities. To be sure the world seemed to
me beautiful and desirable, but it was also filled with vague and
incomprehensible perils. Therefore I always wanted to know at
the start to what and to whom I was entrusting myself. Was this
perhaps connected with my mother, who had abandoned me for
several months? When, as I shall describe later, my neurotic
fainting spells began, the doctor forbade me to engage in gymnastics, much to my satisfaction. I was rid of that burden – and
had swallowed another defeat.

The time thus gained was not spent solely on play. It permitted
me to indulge somewhat more freely the absolute craving I had

developed to read every scrap of printed matter that fell into my hands.

My twelfth year was indeed a fateful one for me. One day in the early summer of 1887 I was standing in the cathedral square, waiting for a classmate who went home by the same route as myself. It was twelve o'clock, and the morning classes were over. Suddenly another boy gave me a shove that knocked me off my feet. I fell, striking my head against the kerbstones so hard that I almost lost consciousness. For about half an hour afterwards I was a little dazed. At the moment I felt the blow the thought flashed through my mind: 'Now you won't have to go to school any more.' I was only half unconscious but I remained lying there a few moments longer than was strictly necessary, chiefly in order to avenge myself on my assailant. Then people picked me up and took me to a house nearby, where two elderly spinster aunts lived.

From then on I began to have fainting spells whenever I had to return to school, and whenever my parents set me to doing my homework. For more than six months I stayed away from school, and for me that was a picnic. I was free, could dream for hours, be anywhere I liked, in the woods or by the water, or draw. I resumed my battle pictures and furious scenes of war, of old castles that were being assaulted or burned, or drew page upon page of caricature. Similar caricatures sometimes appear to me before falling asleep to this day, grinning masks that constantly move and change, among them familiar faces of people who soon afterwards died.

Above all I was able to plunge into the world of the mysterious. To that realm belonged trees, a pool, the swamp, stones and animals, and my father's library. But I was growing more and more away from the world, and had all the while faint pangs of conscience. I frittered away my time with loafing, collecting, reading, and playing. But I did not feel any happier for it; I had the obscure feeling that I was fleeing from myself.

I forgot completely how all this had come about, but I pitied my parents' worries. They consulted various doctors, who scratched their heads and packed me off to spend the holidays with relatives in Winterthur. This city had a railroad station that proved a source of endless delight to me. But when I returned home everything was as before. One doctor thought I had epilepsy. I knew what epileptic fits were like and inwardly laughed at such nonsense. My parents became more worried than ever. Then one day a friend called on my father. They were sitting in the garden and I hid behind a shrub, for I was possessed of an insatiable curiosity. I heard the visitor saying to my father, 'And how is your son?' 'Ah, that's a sad business,' my father replied. 'The doctors no longer know what is wrong with him. They think it may be epilepsy. It would be dreadful if he were incurable. I have lost what little I had, and what will become of the boy if he cannot earn his own living?'

I was thunderstruck. This was the collision with reality. 'Why, then, I must get to work!' I thought suddenly.

From that moment on I became a serious child. I crept away, went to my father's study, took out my Latin grammar, and began to cram with intense concentration. After ten minutes of this I had the finest of fainting fits. I almost fell off the chair, but after a few minutes I felt better and went on working. 'Devil take it, I'm not going to faint,' I told myself, and persisted in my purpose. This time it took about fifteen minutes before the second attack came. That, too, passed like the first. 'And now you must really get to work!' I stuck it out, and after an hour came the third attack. Still I did not give up, and worked for another hour, until I had the feeling that I had overcome the attacks. Suddenly I felt better than I had in all the months before. And in fact the attacks did not recur. From that day on I worked over my grammar and other schoolbooks every day. A few weeks later I returned to school and never suffered another attack, even there. The whole bag of tricks was over and done with! That was when I learned what a neurosis is.

Gradually the recollection of how it had all come about returned to me, and I saw clearly that I myself had arranged this whole disgraceful situation. That was why I had never been seriously angry with the schoolmate who pushed me over. I knew that he had been put up to it, so to speak, and that the whole affair was a diabolical plot on my part. I knew, too, that this was never going to happen to me again. I had a feeling of rage against myself and made a fool of myself in my own eyes. Nobody else was to blame; I was the cursed renegade! From then on I could no longer endure my parents' worrying about me or speaking of me in a pitying tone.

The neurosis became another of my secrets, but it was a shameful secret. A defeat. Nevertheless it induced in me a studied punctiliousness and an unusual diligence. Those days saw the beginnings of my conscientiousness, practised not for the sake of appearances, so that I would amount to something, but for my own sake. Regularly I would get up at five o'clock in order to study, and sometimes I worked from three in the morning till seven, before going to school.

What had led me astray during the crisis was my passion for being alone, my delight in solitude. Nature seemed to me full of wonders, and I wanted to steep myself in them. Every stone, every plant, every single thing seemed alive and indescribably marvellous. I immersed myself in nature, crawled, as it were, into the very essence of nature and away from the whole human world.

I had another important experience at about this time. I was taking the long road to school from Klein-Huningen, where we lived, to Basel, when suddenly for a single moment I had the overwhelming impression of having just emerged from a dense cloud. I knew all at once: now I am *myself*! It was as if a wall of mist were at my back, and behind that wall there was not yet an 'I'. But at this moment *I came upon myself*. Previously I had existed too, but everything had merely happened to me. Now I happened to myself. Now I knew: I am myself now, now I exist. Previously I had been willed to do this and that; now *I* willed. This experience seemed to me tremendously important and new: there was 'authority' in me. . . .

9. Herbert Read:
The Contrary Experience

Herbert Read (1893–1968) was born into a farming family in Yorkshire. At ten, on the death of his father, his family was forced to leave the farm and he began attending a dismal boarding-school outside Halifax. Later he attended the University of Leeds. After the First World War, in which he played an active part, recording the experience in many of his poems, Herbert Read returned to play a leading part in cultural life. He championed modern art (particularly Paul Nash, Ben Nicholson and Henry Moore) and the principle of Romanticism in Literature. He is buried near his birthplace in the churchyard at Kirkdale with the words 'Knight, Poet, Anarchist' inscribed on his grave.

Herbert Read began work on *The Innocent Eye* in 1933. This small densely concentrated sketch subsequently formed the opening section to his longer autobiographical work *The Contrary Experience* (1966).

In his Preface to his autobiography Herbert Read stated that the aim of the book was to delineate 'the growth of a poet's mind in a confusing period of history'. He also claimed that 'as mankind drifted to destruction' the only possible protest was to cultivate one's individuality.

THE VALE

When I went to school I learned that the Vale in which we lived had once been a lake, but long ago the sea had eaten through the hills in the east and so released the fresh waters, leaving a fertile plain. But such an idea would have seemed strange to my innocent mind, so remote was this menacing sea. Our farm was towards the western end of the Vale, and because all our land was as flat as once the surface of the lake had been, we could see around us the misty hills, the Moors to the north, the Wolds to the south, meeting dimly in the east where they were more distant. This rim of hills was nearest in the south, at least in effect; for as the sun sank in the west the windows of Stamper's farm in the south caught the blazing rays and cast them back at us, continually drawing our eyes in that direction. But we never travelled so far south as those hills; for the Church and the Market, the only outer places of pilgrimage, lay to the north, five or six miles away. By habit we faced north: the south was 'behind'.

I seemed to live, therefore, in a basin, wide and shallow like the milkpans in the dairy; but the even bed of it was checkered with pastures and cornfields, and the rims were the soft blues and purples of the moorlands. This basin was my world, and I had no inkling of any larger world, for no strangers came to us out of it, and we never went into it. Very rarely my father went to York or Northallerton, to buy a piece of machinery for the farm or to serve on a jury at the Assizes; but only our vague wonder accompanied him, and the toys he brought back with him might have come, like sailors' curios, from Arabia or Cathay. The basin at times was very wide, especially in the clearness of a summer's day; but as dusk fell it would suddenly contract, the misty hills would draw near, and with night they had clasped us close: the centre of the world had become a candle shining from the kitchen window. Inside, in the sitting-room where we spent most of our life, a lamp was lit, with a round glass shade like a full yellow moon. There we were bathed before the fire, said our prayers kneeling on the hearthrug, and then disappeared up the steep stairs lighted by a candle to bed; and once there, the world was finally blotted out. I think it returned with the same suddenness, at least in summer; but the waking world was a new world, a hollow cube with light streaming in from one window across to a large bed holding, as the years went by, first one, then two, and finally three boys, overseen by two Apostles from one wall and adjured from another, above a chest of drawers, by a white pottery plaque within a pink-lustre frame, printed with a vignette of an angel blowing a trumpet and the words:

PRAISE YE THE LORD

Sometimes the child's mind went on living even during the darkness of night, listening to the velvet stillness of the fields. The stillness of a sleeping town, of a village, is nothing to the stillness of a remote farm; for the peace of day in such a place is so kindly that the ear is attuned to the subtlest sounds, and time is slow. If by chance a cow should low in the night it is like the abysmal cry of some hellish beast, bringing woe to the world. And who knows what hellish beasts might roam by night, for in the cave by the Church five miles away they once found the bones of many strange animals, wolves and hyaenas, and even the tusks of mammoths. The night-sound that still echoes in my mind, however, is not of this kind: it is gentler and more musical – the distant sound of horse-hooves on the highroad, at first dim and uncertain, but growing louder until they more suddenly cease. To that distant sound, I realized later, I must have come into the world, for the doctor arrived on horseback at four o'clock one December morning to find me uttering my first shriek.

I think I heard those hooves again the night my father died, but of this I am not certain; perhaps I shall remember when I come to relate that event, for now the memory of those years, which end shortly after my tenth birthday, comes fitfully, when the proper associations are aroused. If only I can recover the sense and uncertainty of those innocent years, years in which we seemed not so much to live as to be lived by forces outside us, by the wind and trees and moving clouds and all the mobile engines of our expanding world – then I am convinced I shall possess a key to much that has happened to me in this other world of conscious living. The echoes of my life which I find in my early childhood are too many to be dismissed as vain coincidences; but it is perhaps my conscious life which is the echo, the only real experiences in life being those lived with a virgin sensibility – so that we only hear a tone once, only see a colour once, see, hear, touch, taste and smell everything but once, the first time. All life is an echo of our first sensations, and we build up our consciousness, our whole mental life, by variations and combinations of these elementary sensations. But it is more complicated than that, for the senses apprehend not only colours and tones and shapes, but also patterns and atmospheres, and our first discovery of these determines the larger patterns and subtler atmospheres of all our subsequent existence.

THE FARM

I have given the impression that the Farm was remote, but this is not strictly true. Not half a mile on each side of us was another farmhouse, and clustering near the one to the east were three or four cottages. We formed, therefore, a little community, remote as such; in 'Doomsday Book' we had been described as a hamlet. The nearest village was two or three miles away, but to the south, so that it did not count for much until we began to go to school, which was not until towards the end of the period of which I write. Northwards our farm road ran through two fields and then joined the highroad running east and west; but eastward this road soon turned into a road running north and south, down which we turned northwards again, to the Church five miles away, and to Kirby, our real metropolis, six miles away.

The farmhouse was a square stone box with a roof of vivid red tiles; its front was to the south, and warm enough to shelter some apricot trees against the wall. But there was no traffic that way: all our exits and entrances were made on the north side, through the kitchen; and I think even our grandest visitors did not disdain that approach. Why should they? On the left as they entered direct into the kitchen was an old oak dresser; on the right a large open fireplace, with a great iron kettle hanging from the reckan, and an oven to the near side of it. A long deal table, glistening with a honey gold sheen from much scrubbing, filled the far side of the room; long benches ran down each side of it. The floor was flagged with stone, each stone neatly outlined with a border of some softer yellow stone, rubbed on after every washing. Sides of bacon and plum-dusky hams hung from the beams of the wooden ceiling.

By day it was the scene of intense bustle. The kitchenmaid

was down by five o'clock to light the fire; the labourers crept
down in stockinged feet and drew on their heavy boots; they lit
candles in their horn lanthorns and went out to the cattle. Breakfast was at seven, dinner at twelve, tea at five. Each morning of
the week had its appropriate activity: Monday was washing day,
Tuesday ironing, Wednesday and Saturday baking, Thursday
'turning out' upstairs and churning, Friday 'turning out' downstairs. Every day there was the milk to skim in the dairy – the
dairy was to the left of the kitchen, and as big as any other room
in the house. The milk was poured into large flat pans and allowed
to settle; it was skimmed with horn scoops, like toothless combs.

At dinner, according to the time of the year, there would be
from five to seven farm labourers, the two servant girls, and the
family, with whom, for most of the time, there was a governess – a
total of from ten to fifteen mouths to feed every day. The bustle
reached its height about midday; the men would come in and sit
on the dresser, swinging their legs impatiently; when the food was
served, they sprang to the benches and ate in solid gusto, like
animals. They disappeared as soon as the pudding had been
served, some to smoke a pipe in the saddle room, others to do
work which could not wait. Then all the clatter of washing up
rose and subsided. More peaceful occupations filled the afternoon.
The crickets began to sing in the hearth. The kettle boiled for tea.
At nightfall a candle was lit, the foreman or the shepherd sat
smoking in the armchair at the fireside end of the table. The latch
clicked as the others came in one by one and went early to bed.

The kitchen was the scene of many events which afterwards
flowed into my mind from the pages of books. Whenever in a
tale a belated traveller saw a light and came through the darkness
to ask for shelter, it was to this kitchen door. I can no longer
identify the particular stories, but they do not belong to this period
of childhood so much as to my later boyhood and youth, long
after I had left the Farm; and even today my first memories easily
usurp the function of the imagination, and clothe in familiar
dimensions and patterns, exact and objective, the scenes which
the romancer has purposely left vague. Perhaps the effect of all
romance depends on this faculty we have of giving our own
definition to the fancies of others. A mind without memories
means a body without sensibility; our memories make our
imaginative life, and it is only as we increase our memories,
widening the imbricated shutters which divide our mind from the
light, that we find with quick recognition those images of truth

which the world is pleased to attribute to our creative gift.

THE GREEN

The Green, a space of about an acre, lay in front of the kitchen door. It was square; one side, that to the left as we came out of the house, was fully taken up by a range of sheds. A shorter range of buildings continued in line with the house on the right – first the saddle-room, one of my favourite haunts, then the shed where the dog-kart and buggy were kept, and finally the blacksmith's shop. Beyond this were the grindstones and the ash-heap (in just such a heap, I imagined, Madame Curie discovered radium) and then a high hedge led to the corner of the Green, where three enormous elm-trees, the only landmark near our farm, overhung the duck-pond. On the other two sides the Green was bounded by hedges. The farm-road led past the sheds and then to the left through the stackyard; to the right there was a cart-track leading across the fields to the next farm with its cluster of cottages.

Our dominion was really four-fold: the Green I have just described, and then three other almost equal squares, the one to the left of the Green being the farm outhouses, a rectangular court of low buildings enclosing the Fodgarth, or fold-garth, and two others to the south of the house, the orchard to the east, the garden to the west. Each province was perfectly distinct, divided off by high walls or hedges; and each had its individual powers or mysteries. The Green was the province of water and of fowl, of traffic and trade, the only province familiar to strangers – to the postman and the pedlar, and the scarlet huntsmen. In winter we made the snowman there; in summer avoided its shelterless waste. On Mondays the washed clothes flapped in the wind, but for the rest of the week it was willingly resigned to hens, ducks, geese, guinea fowls, and turkeys – whose discursive habits, incidentally, made it no fit playground for children. The pond was more attractive, but because of its stagnation it could not compete with the becks not far away. I remember it best in a hot summer, when the water dried up and left a surface of shining mud, as smooth as moleskin, from which projected the rusty wrecks of old cans and discarded implements. Perhaps it was a forbidden area; it serves no purpose in my memory.

The pump was built over a deep well, in the corner of the Green near the kitchen; it was too difficult for a boy to work.

One day, underneath the stones which took the drip, we discovered bright green lizards. Behind the pump, handy to the
water, was the copper-house – the 'copper' being a large cauldron
built in over a furnace. Here the clothes were boiled on a Monday;
here, too, potatoes for the pigs were boiled in their earthy skins,
and the pigs were not the only little animals who enjoyed them,
for they are delicious when cooked in this way. Outside the same
copper-house the pigs were killed, to be near the cauldron of
boiling water with which they were scalded. The animal was
drawn from its sty by a rope through the ring in its nose: its
squealing filled the whole farm till it reached the copper-house,
and there by the side of a trestle its throat was cut with a sharp
knife and the hot blood gushed on to the ground. The carcass was
then stretched on the trestle, and the whole household joined in
the work of scraping the scalded hide: it was done with metal
candlesticks, the hollow foot making a sharp and effective instrument for removing the bristles and outer skin. The carcass was
then disembowelled and dismembered. The copper was once more
requisitioned to render down the superfluous fat, which was first
cut into dice. The remnants of this process, crisp shreds known as
scraps, formed our favourite food for days afterwards. In fact,
pig-killing was followed by a whole orgy of good things to eat –
pork-pies, sausages and pigs'-feet filling the bill for a season. But
the scenes I have described, and many others of the same nature,
such as the searing of horses' tails, the killing of poultry, the
birth of cattle, even the lewdness of a half-witted labourer, were
witnessed by us children with complete passivity – just as I have
seen children of the same age watching a bull-fight in Spain quite
unmoved by its horrors. Pity, and even terror, are emotions which
develop when we are no longer innocent, and the sentimental
adult who induces such emotions in the child is probably breaking
through defences which nature has wisely put round the tender
mind. The child even has a natural craving for horrors. He
survives just because he is without sentiment, for only in this way
can his green heart harden sufficiently to withstand the wounds
that wait for it.

On the south side of the Green were two familiar shrines,
each with its sacred fire. The first was the saddle-room, with its
pungent clean smell of saddle-soap. It was a small whitewashed
room, hung with bright bits and stirrups and long loops of
leather reins; the saddles were in a loft above, reached by a
ladder and trap-door. In the middle was a small cylindrical stove,

kept burning through the winter, and making a warm friendly shelter where we could play undisturbed. Our chief joy was to make lead shot, or bullets as we called them; and for this purpose there existed a long-handled crucible and a mould. At what now seems to me an incredibly early age we melted down the strips of lead we found in the window-sill, and poured the sullen liquid into the small aperture of the mould, which was in the form of a pair of pincers – closed whilst the pouring was in progress. When opened, the gleaming silver bullets, about the size of a pea, fell out of the matrix and rolled away to cool on the stone floor. We used the bullets in our catapults, but the joy was in the making of them, and in the sight of their shining beauty.

The blacksmith's shop was a still more magical shrine. The blacksmith came for a day periodically, to shoe or re-shoe the horses, to repair wagons and make simple implements. In his dusky cave the bellows roared, the fire was blown to a white intensity, and then suddenly the bellows-shaft was released and the soft glowing iron drawn from the heart of the fire. Then clang clang clang on the anvil, the heavenly shower of ruby and golden sparks, and our precipitate flight to a place of safety. All around us, in dark cobwebbed corners, were heaps of old iron, discarded horseshoes, hoops and pipes. Under the window was a tank of water for slaking and tempering the hot iron, and this water possessed the miraculous property of curing warts.

In these two shrines I first experienced the joy of making things. Everywhere around me the earth was stirring with growth and the beasts were propagating their kind. But these wonders passed unobserved by my childish mind, unrecorded in memory. They depended on forces beyond our control, beyond my conception. But fire was real, and so was the skill with which we shaped hard metals to our design and desire.

III From Students' Autobiographies

The following passages from students' autobiographies have been loosely arranged to suggest the development of experience. The early passages tend to concentrate on memories of infancy and childhood, the later passages on the memories of adolescence. Where I have decided to quote a whole autobiography or a very lengthy extract I have had to depart a little from this guiding principle. I would also like to point out that a few names have been changed to ensure anonymity.

My Life

1. THE HOUSE

It was an old house, very large, very dirty and it was situated opposite a cemetery. I never liked it because it made me feel lost and lonely. Its bigness was accentuated by the fact that there was very little furniture in it and that we had was old and cumbersome. It was always dark and the sun never seemed to penetrate it.

Most of it was a mystery to me. The idea of the cellar with its very own brand of creepy-crawly within tended to scare me and the box room, whose very name sounded mysterious, was absolutely taboo. I preferred not to think about what it might contain and I knew there was a reason why it came between my parents' bedroom and mine but this reason also tended to get pushed to the back of my mind.

But it was my bedroom which was undoubtedly the most loathsome in the entire house. It was more immense than the other rooms and twice as dark. I was not allowed to leave the landing light on until I began to sleepwalk and after this the one shaft of light through the door was a constant comfort to me.

If the upper floor of the house was decidedly sinister then the lower one was a constant reminder of sickness. Mother lay on the couch down there for several weeks, Father came home with a heavily bandaged hand and a white face once when we were playing nurses and I had to lie in darkness there when I had a sweating, shaking fever.

There was one safe place in the house and that was under the table where I spent a great deal of time doing nothing in particular, except listening. A woman came into the room once; she wore black and she was speaking in a harsh voice to my mother, who was crying. In fright I ran behind the couch and stayed there until she went away.

2. THE SCHOOL

There are two things about my infants school which stand out for opposite reasons. One is the climbing frame in the classroom and the other the Wendy House behind which was the dressing-up box.

The climbing frame was always symbolic of fear and hatred to me, the Wendy House and dressing-up box pure delight and security.

Quite frequently we were made to go up the climbing frame in order to get some physical exercise. Most of the girls clambered up without any trouble probably because they were taller than I, but I used to wait till last. The thing looked so large and unsafe to me and my knees trembled before I even put my foot on the first rung. To make it worse the tallest, biggest-boned girl in the class used to sit on the platform at the top looking down at me like someone who had just climbed Everest sneering at me for my slowness. Not being very fond of showing people I was scared, I used to climb shakily up and every rung seemed a mile away but I would never get onto the top. Adrienne would hold out her hand to me to pull me up but by that time I was already on the descent.

I was always first into the hall to get to the Wendy House. I shut the door on the world and there I stayed until I was practically dragged out. There was a small table in there, two tiny chairs, a red plastic tea-set, some dolls and the dressing-up box. I spent hours in those large hats with pins in them, long silk dresses and stiletto-heeled shoes pretending to be the teacher, the neighbour and other characters well known to me then, mimicking their voices, their walks, doing what I thought they would do and say in certain situations, using the dolls as victims and *becoming* them. Yes, Wendy House time was always too soon over for me then it was back to the pencils and tidy boxes and sums. Sometimes when we had silent reading I imagined I was a character in the story but it didn't compare with actually dressing up.

When the time came for me to leave and go to a new school, the only thing I regretted parting with was that Wendy House, and the climbing frame loomed up in all its ugliness whenever I felt sad about going.

3. THE JUNIOR SCHOOL

My early life seems relatively unimportant in comparison to what I am now to relate. If most people were asked what they thought had been the greatest influence on them, they would answer 'parents'. School was my greatest influence, both junior and senior, although my parents had much to do with my actions at school.

Byron Street was much larger than my infants school and once inside it seemed that one was practically imprisoned. It was here that I realised I was part of a whole universe and no longer my own tiny secure one of books and conversations with myself.

At first I withdrew and grew into books without much opposition, although my teacher sometimes rapped my knuckles for non-concentration. I was often bored, so, though I could keep up with the work, my refusal to try caused me to take the lower positions in exams supporting the rest, so to speak.

The announcement that I was to enter the 'B' stream was a turning point. My parents were upset and thought I could do better. I could not fathom out why they should be worried but their faces impressed something on my mind and determined to do better I eventually warranted a place in the 'A's.

I worked hard, especially at my writing, and was often proud to hear the teacher read out my work in class. One essay which began 'the doorknob turned slowly in the lock' brought many nods of approval.

I made friends in whom I more or less completely confided, rather than my parents. Not only were my parents unimpressed by my improved report cards, they were also very concerned about what other people thought of me. They rarely helped me although my father sometimes helped me with maths about which I shed many a tear screaming 'I can't do it' and Dad would say 'No such thing as can't – more like won't'.

Because my parents were so concerned about what others thought of me, I boasted, romanced and held impromptu performances for my friends but I ceased to tell my parents anything about school and even when I was in serious trouble I kept it dark. In short, I became two people.

I felt a failure in the fourth year and was told I would not get my eleven plus because of my non-performance in maths. Instead I painted with gusto and put on small plays which I scripted myself from books, often getting angry when my friends did things wrong, calling them names and stamping, with the teacher looking on and laughing.

When we were herded into the hall to take the eleven plus I had a tight feeling in my stomach and it seemed important to do well though exactly why I did not know. When the results came out I fainted into the row behind. My parents gave me five pounds but few words were spoken.

One of the saddest experiences in my life was leaving that school. The words of the hymn 'The day thou gavest Lord is ended' were all around me. I could not sing. Even the red-headed bully who had often threatened me with torture was like a God. Only darkness faced me now. I walked through the gates and cried all the way home.

4. GRAMMAR SCHOOL

It was here that my character, already starting to form at junior school, fully developed. It was a big, dark, gloomy school which people used to call 'the hospital'. There were air-raid shelters all along the front, lots of fields and many out-buildings where, in later years, we used to have a quiet smoke.

The feeling of being insignificant and unimportant was increased by the size of the school. I wandered around in my navy blue uniform, just like all the others, looking at the older girls, the seemingly endless corridors and the cloakroom pegs; feeling like a very tiny fish in a whole sea of bigger fish for the whole of my first year and secretly hating every minute of it.

The only way in which I had a chance to distinguish myself

was with my classmates. The very first day when my name was called out I went out to the front and tripped over a satchel which caused an uproar of laughter from the rest of the girls and from then on I was regarded as a 'good laugh'. Naturally I played up to this and became popular. I did very little work for the first three years in my school career. I spent my time getting in scrapes, dodging games and playing practical jokes on the teachers, disrupting their lessons.

I told my parents very little about what I did at school. At home I was quiet and sneaky, at school loud and ridiculous.

It was lucky that there was one teacher in the school who recognised that I had worth – the drama teacher. She urged me to join the dramatic society and I did. From then on my attitudes at school changed. I became interested in something academic. My interest in this one thing caught on in other school activities. I suddenly became nothing short of a swot. This however had repercussions for although I pleased my teachers, I lost the favour of most of my friends. Instead of laughing at my antics they sneered. Whenever we read a play aloud in class and I took a part, I loved it but dreaded it at the same time. Their faces wore queer expressions. They hated me for taking it all seriously.

At first I took no notice. I was content with just one or two close friends around me, but later I became angry about it. The vast amounts of nervous energy I had previously got rid of by acting the fool had built up inside me forming a great block of hurt, anger and extreme sensitivity. I was like a bomb ready to go off at the slightest uncareful word or look. I became emotional and serious both at home and at school. At home I was made to feel bad if I had emotional outbursts but at school they did not come down upon them quite so heavily. Once in a school play I had one of my outbursts at a girl who had thrown me out by giving me the wrong cue and the drama teacher only calmed me down without telling me off. In the sixth form when I was having extra emotional problems which I felt I could not express at home, these outbursts became more frequent and were often directed at the teachers.

Despite all this my schooldays will always be remembered with a mixture of disgust and delight. Summer is one of the good things, lying on the grass talking of the past and the future with a few close friends, wondering what we were going to be – sharing things together and verbally.

So I got my 'O' levels and went on into the sixth without a

second thought. They were dismal years. The common room was a hovel with a tea urn and a bowl of slops underneath it, dirty cups and mucky chairs. We seemed to have done little in these years but smoke and discuss. I became more sensitive because I no longer had time for drama, a pale individual with long, scruffy hair.

On my last day we all promised to keep in touch. I turned at the gate to take a parting look. I felt nothing. The sun was shining. I was free.

5. RECENTLY – AND SUICIDE

When I left home it was raining. I pressed my nose against the window pane and looked out. The taxi came, a wet kiss on the forehead and away. The train was saying free, free, free. I was free. I was one person, no longer two. I could do what I liked and I did.

My parents knew nothing about what I did at college. An unfortunate relationship with a man, my clothes, my new attitudes. When I needed help, I had to help myself – they mustn't know about me. At first this was fine but that term, that dreadful term was different.

Tiredness, exhaustion, confusion, brain working overtime, sleeping pills, men, unkind people. I was going down and I couldn't get up. Trying to spread out but getting crushed in. I was crushed. At the same time I fell in love. I needed him, he wouldn't help.

It happened so quickly, the dance, the rain, the pills; then darkness, oblivion, and a gradual return to life.

My parents did not know me till that moment but they do now. They helped me back to my feet, supported me on loving crutches. Perhaps my life would have been so much different if they had known me and I would not be what I am. It's too late to repair but it's early days to understand myself.

The Time When Everything Changed

She sat and thought but memories still seemed to elude her grasp, a feeling that a mistlike curtain withheld the truth. If she could only reach out and tear the curtain apart, then the knowledge of things done and words spoken would flood back, like water which has for too long been kept behind a dam. But there was always this feeling that she had never existed before, that all that had gone before was but a dream. She wondered about that for a while, was childhood but a dream, a trance-like state in which one only lives in the imagination, for surely she had never been anyone else but herself so why couldn't she remember who she was? The doctor had assured them that it was quite natural, after all the child had been very close to her brother. It would pass, and if it didn't, well, it didn't really matter did it? But it *did* matter, it mattered to the child who sat in the corner thinking. No one realized this, not even the child herself until she was older and sat down and tried as she had done many years before to remember.

Then she realised from whence came this feeling of detachment she carried around with her like a shield held between her and the world and through which only one person had ever penetrated.

It came from the time when everything changed, from when she became an adult, not physically, nor in the eyes of grown-ups, but mentally. This time stood out in her memory, the actual day or year she didn't remember, just the incident, the people standing round in groups whispering, growing silent whenever she came near, the darkened room which she must not enter because it was there.

'Mummy, mummy, I want to go to my bedroom.'

'All right, all right, go upstairs, but you must walk quickly through the front room and not look at anything inside.'

The child walked towards the door and turned the handle, quickly pushed open the door and shut it behind her. Looking neither to left nor right, she marched sturdily towards the door that led to the stairs. She opened the door but as she turned to close it behind her, in the shaft of light from the hall she saw it, a long narrow wooden box. She opened the other door and dashed quickly up the stairs to her bedroom. Once there she threw herself upon the bed, body heaving with emotion.

She got up and went to make a cup of coffee. Yes, that was the time when everything changed, the time when her brother died and she started turning into herself, a reserve which she realized now would always be an intrinsic part of herself.

Not that she could remember him, so she could not really be said to miss him. Of course as she had grown older she realised what had happened, people told her things, and she almost convinced herself that she remembered the incidents which they fondly recounted, but inside herself she knew that it was a sham.

Her mind switched on to a completely different tack – amazing the ways that things influenced your life without you realising it. If things hadn't happened as they did she wouldn't be the person she was. Those few short months had been the most traumatic of her life.

Afterwards she was always apart from the others, she held herself apart. She had a secret, a terrible secret, that had been impressed upon her. No one must know.

On consideration, she decided that it was this, the second incident, that had had the most profound effect upon her, the one involving her sister. At that time, she now realised, it had been a shameful occurrence to have a baby when one wasn't married, especially when the father was already married and couldn't marry you. So Maureen was sent to an aunt in the country and the child and her mother went to visit her every week. The story was that Maureen had gone to work as a receptionist in a hotel in another part of the country. No one thought this strange as she had done so before.

This time however the girl kept thinking someone was going to come up to her and shout, 'your sister's going to have a baby'; she didn't know why she was afraid of this. There seemed to be no reason for such a fear but inside she knew that no one else should know, as she hugged the secret to herself and lost herself in a world of fantasy, a world peopled with fictional characters, in which she was the heroine, good, beautiful and intelligent.

She rarely played with the other children now, preferring to sit in a corner reading.

Separation and Reunion

My first recollection of childhood was at the age of three when my parents left me in the care of my aunt, owing to my grandfather's death. I was then the only child so naturally I was spoilt at home but at my Aunt Amelia's I was pushed into the background, for I was now one of two. She disliked me and I her, which made me long for my home and family, but Howard my cousin would comfort me when I cried for my mother. Every day I would religiously ask if my mother was coming for me, hoping that it would make her return, but she didn't appear.

A week later I was playing on the path when suddenly I saw a stranger coming towards me. I stared at the approaching figure, who looked very familiar but who was she? The stranger was now bending towards me and suddenly I realised who it was – my mother!

I was never the same after my short stay at Aunt Amelia's because I became inseparable from my mother. I would follow her everywhere and cling to her when strange people called at the house. Most of all, I feared night and would try to stay up as long as possible to avoid being alone. For reassurance that my parents were still downstairs, I would shout for trivial things and cry. Many an hour my father would sit at my bedside, holding my hand and watch me go to sleep. Just being able to feel his soft, warm hand in mine was enough to make me happy and content that they were still with me.

It was obvious mother was perturbed about my sudden inwardness and she would spend hours in making me a new party dress, hopefully thinking I'd go to my friends' birthday parties. She would carefully get me ready but when it came to her leaving me at my friend's house, I would cry and would desperately want to be taken back home. As the last resort I was taken to Sunday School, which I loathed. Once again I would collapse into tears if mother left the room, so she quietly sat at the back of the classroom and listened to the story which was being told.

The Garden, the Pond, the House and the School

The garden at our first house is perhaps my earliest memory. Large and quiet with as many secret places as any child could hope for, that is how I remember it. At the very bottom there was a small orchard which was 'my' part of the garden, through a hole in the hedge I could get from the orchard into a field behind the house. In this field there was a smelly, dried-up pond decorated with broken planks. This was the inevitable destination of all my rambles. I spent hours at that pond, playing usually with my brother Ian, sometimes with the other children who lived nearby.

One winter when that pond froze over, my brother broke his

arm there. The two of us were sliding on it. We had been keeping to the edge, but my brother, who always had the ability to make a fool of himself when trying to prove a point, went across the middle. The ice was too thin and he went straight through! The water itself was only about two feet deep but he fell awkwardly and broke his arm just above the elbow. At the time neither of us knew it was broken and Ian made me promise I wouldn't tell our parents as he was supposed to be going up to Edinburgh to stay with my grandparents two days after. He went, with a broken arm and no one knew. For a fortnight he went round and then he collapsed in the middle of Edinburgh. It took nearly seven months for that arm to mend. I blamed myself for the pain and discomfort he suffered and, though my parents tried to make me understand it was not my fault, I have always felt guilty for the two weeks of pain my brother went through.

I was only six when that happened and we left Huyten the next summer. I didn't go to that pond again.

The orchard consisted of about twenty trees, mostly apple trees with damp green furry trunks. There was one huge pear tree as well. I cannot remember that tree in any other way than covered in creamy blossom. In between the orchard and the lawn was a greenhouse. Not a well-kept one, but an old one with broken panes and ancient tomato plants. One day when I would be about five years old, I found a family of mice there – all dead. I remember we had had Beatrix Potter read to us at school and I cried my eyes out over those mice. I made my father bury them and my parents and my brother and myself held a funeral service for them. I picked dandelions for their grave for weeks.

The rest of the garden was made up of a large lawn, rhododendron bushes and a small rose garden which separated the lawn from a stone patio. The wall round the rose garden had little pillars at the corners and on the top of these were small stone animals. I can't remember what they were exactly. I don't think I ever knew. They were too old and too crumbled for me to recognise any particular animal but Ian and I had named them all: one was called 'Bill' and one which I think originally was a lion went by the name – most unregal – of 'Pongo'.

I loved that garden. I loved Sunday mornings there when my father would mess around trying to grow things. The strange thing was that after dark the garden would lose all its familiarity and become terrifyingly alien and threatening.

The house itself was an ordinary semi-detached with a long

narrow hallway and a passage leading to the kitchen. In the kitchen was an old table which had been scarred and battered by a Labrador puppy that I only vaguely remember, as he was stolen only a few months after we bought him. The table I do remember; all four legs showed vivid ochre scars against the darker stained wood where the puppy had clawed and chewed at it.

My left leg still shows a scar where I also had been clawed and chewed when trying to put a pair of my brother's shorts on the puppy. That is the only clear memory I have of that particular dog. The next dog we had, also a Labrador, put up no resistance at all when I dressed him up in anything that was available.

I went to school when I was four and a half years old – at Easter. The school was very small – just a large room that could be divided by a screen, another classroom, a kitchen and cloak-rooms. One very clear memory I have of it is the front door, which seemed huge. In fact, it was an old oak panelled door with brass studs all over it and a 'Green Man' door knocker. The smell of plastic tablecloths always conjures up a picture of the kitchen at the school. There were only about twenty of us and we all had morning milk and biscuits and lunch together round a long table covered with a blue plastic tablecloth. It had flowers on it and I spent more time pulling the plastic away where the petals should have been than eating.

I remember being very happy living in Huyten; it was still a relatively small quiet village when we were there. I can't remember when it ever rained or when I ever cried.

Early Memories

The farthest back that I can go in my memory is between the ages of two-and-a-half and three years, the period immediately prior to my mother's death from cancer. There was a day when a large, beautiful deckchair arrived complete with foot-stool and canopy, the purpose of which was to help my mother 'convalesce'. I distinctly remember my father saying that to me, though she was obviously not going to recover. On that occasion the door into the room where my mother lay, which was off the hall passage, was slightly ajar and I peeped in to see her staring rather blankly at the ceiling. I do not remember her death or being upset and wondering what was happening but can remember asking where she had gone, my father replying that she was in Heaven. I think I was vaguely puzzled at this but can remember no more of my feelings.

My father, my brother and myself then moved to the house of my Auntie Jess, herself at the time recently widowed with one daughter, Christine, about thirteen years old. I seem to have a blank spot here, for little springs to memory from this period though I think it contained the seeds of much trouble later on. My father, obviously deeply stunned and grieved, my brother a child of seven, detached from his mother at a very impressionable age, my aunt, also in a state of grief, and my cousin having to cope with adolescent difficulties as well as her own grief at her father's death; all these cannot have made a favourable home background. Indeed my brother, even at this time, started going off on his own for whole days, travelling up and down the lines of the underground, losing contact with my father and fostering deep-seated resentment at my mother's death. My brother, four years my senior, has never recovered from this upheaval in his life. He has always actively hated my stepmother, has gone away from the family as much as possible throughout his growing years – he was out on fishing trawlers, getting in with rough seamen in his school holidays at about the age of fifteen. This separation of his original background from his developing years, due to lack of trust on his part, and lack of understanding on the part of others, has left him a blunt, unsociable creature, lacking in courtesy and unconcerned for others around him.

One memory I do have is of a particular dream, which recurred several times – a short episode in which I sank back, tired, onto my pillow which turned to a thick, soft mass of cobweb. More distinctly I can remember Sunday School which I was made to attend though neither my father nor my aunt were Christians. There was an occasion when I was shown a famous painting of Christ holding a lantern, as the light of the world. On being asked whom it was in the picture, I replied, after much hesitation, that it was a thief – which created a slight awkwardness in the atmosphere. All this time I can remember little contact with my father.

At the age of four-and-a-half we moved from Essex to Orpington, Kent. At first my brother and I were looked after by housekeepers. The first of these, a Miss Gooding, was if anything a right old battleaxe. She was a Roman Catholic and had a habit of taking me to see the nuns at an orphanage in the vicinity of whom I was very much afraid, and of whose purpose I had not the slightest idea. I remember Miss Gooding also for forcing me to eat dinners which at that time I had no appetite for.

My first school, at which I stayed only a few months until a new school was finished, was very old-fashioned and strict. The only vivid memory I have is of the headmaster storming round the canteen at lunchtime informing the 'little ones' that they should 'eat what they don't like first and eat what they do like after' but allowing the older children the privilege of choosing to eat as they wished.

My next primary school was fairly modern in outlook, though run on the traditional lines of rows of desks and fitting into the routine. I can remember, though, enjoying a few more imaginative pursuits – such as needlework, country dancing and making papier-maché models of the geographical relief of an area. But my overriding impression of primary school is one of fear, especially as I moved higher up the school when the teacher was a real boys' man, as it were, very strict though laughing with the boys, developing a sort of camaraderie between himself and them, which did not include gentleness and an over-sensitivity to the nervous and ill-at-ease child. As far as religion went at this period I can vaguely remember pictures of Old Testament characters on the wall but cannot remember what we were taught. It certainly did not register much – whether that is a good or bad thing is another question, for no doubt the teacher had no special quali-fication to teach the subject. It seems strange that a grammar-school teacher has a qualification to teach the subject, yet at primary school, with children at a very impressionable age, this is not always necessary.

However, school was not a very important aspect of my life as far as I was concerned. I did not really understand why I was going there and cannot remember getting really deep down and embroiled in any subject or project.

When I was between the age of six and seven my father re-married. I never met my stepmother until after their marriage because she was Danish and my father had met her in Denmark. Though my immediate reaction on meeting her was to hug her, we never hit it off because on the surface my stepmother is a cold woman, not very affectionate and rather strict.

I remember from this time a few horrifying dreams which I have never been able to consider without shuddering. Once I dreamt that I was in my bedroom and the light on my ceiling began swinging backwards and forwards, the lead getting longer and longer as the swinging became more violent. Eventually it came away from the ceiling. At arms length I took hold of it and rushed down the stairs, throwing it out of the hall window. My father then told me not to worry about it and to go and sit on the second step of the staircase with my stepmother. Whether I sat on this one or the one beneath it, I cannot quite remember. An obvious interpretation that I was given of this dream is that the light represented my mother, and because it was not switched on she was not important to me. So the light falling down was the final severing of her from myself. Thus the sitting down on the stairs was my acceptance or partial acceptance of my step-mother. There was another dream in which a black book mark I had, in the shape of a long black candle, turned into my step-mother in a long black dress, gliding towards me with a fixed, terrifying expression in her eyes.

Whatever the subconscious results of these dreams, I know that I spent my primary-school days in a rather dream-like manner. School did not concern me, though I cannot think what else did either. One incident I remember, which makes me squirm and which perhaps was a reflection of my state of inner being. Eggs used to really make me feel ill. One day on being made to stay at the table until I had eaten a fried egg, I slyly slipped it under the carpet when everyone had left the room – only to have it dis-covered a couple of weeks later in the presence of a visitor! Though it reflects most terribly on myself, I'm sure no normal child (if there is such a thing) would stoop to such depths. I'm led to wonder if I would be expecting too much of an education, even a religious education, to think it could repair this state that had been produced in me, let alone put something constructive in its place.

Piecing the Fragments

Her earliest memories consisted of short, brief, bright pictures: tea bushes, coolies, brilliant flowers, heat, all merging into a canvas of flat colour. The first concrete memory, incorporating picture, sound and emotion did not come until about three-and-a-half years old. That memory did not need extracting from a whole; it was complete in itself. White – white shorts, white shirt, white socks. She'd demanded that he wear white, as she remembered him, but had forgotten how huge he was. Still, the thought of the surprise they had brought overcame her awe and, grabbing his hand, she dragged him to the cabin. Pointing to a cot on the bunk she said, 'Daddy, look what we've brought you'.

Again and again she probed back, trying to piece the fragments of colour, people, places and warmth into a comprehensible pattern. They merged for a moment, only to be lost again in a shifting mist. Again she reached out and grasped a memory and lost it. What emerged finally, perhaps covered a space of four years, but time itself was irrelevant, as the events could have been separated by minutes, hours or months.

A deep pool, surrounded by rubber trees and bright flowers evoked remembrances of cool, clear water, laughter, grown-up talk, incomprehensible but fascinating. Water – another pool, this time surrounded by concrete, hushed footed servants, the tinkle of glass, glaring heat. Heat – the click of insects, sticky air, hiding amongst bamboo and canvas; warnings of 'don't leave the paths – snakes – they are dangerous'. Snakes – 'Mummy, come quickly'. Funny, she vividly remembered the snake she had seen in her parents' bedroom, but it had slithered onto the verandah by the time they arrived. She hadn't really been worried about snakes anyway, because she had seen the hully-gully man produce them out of his mouth. He used to swallow big stones too and he had a monkey.

She had also had a monkey but somehow one day it disappeared. It was explained that a wild cat had taken it. She didn't much like the idea of wild animals but she liked elephants. They were tame and worked hard. She had watched them bathing, being scrubbed by mahoots and then sluicing themselves down with the river water.

She was suddenly struck by a thought – people. She could not really remember people. They were all there: mother, father, nanny and the house boys; there to love, care for, feed and play with her. She had a sister too. They were always there when she wanted them, so they must have been important, but she could not remember them. Odd to think that the time when people looked after her the most should be the time she remembered them least of all.

So existence flowed on, safely cocooned which created a pure acceptance. The tea factory and the smell of the drying leaves; the rubber factory and the fascinating liquid rubber that could be moulded into a ball and bounced. The glitter of the Perahera, the noise of drums and the music. Playing, laughing, running, talking, crying – crying?

Her thoughts flew from the light to the grey, from the grey to the dark. Lying in a lower bunk in a small cabin, the humid air alive with unfamiliar noises and smells; cries of the natives, the throb of engines, the smell of the sea, corrupted by oil and food odours. Gripped by a tight fist, unable to understand the total misery that engulfed her; wracked by shuddering sobs and aching throat muscles, she lay in her bunk. Why did she have to say goodbye to Nanny? Why had Nanny cried when she put her to bed? Shadowy figures explaining that they were going home, that Nanny couldn't come. Why, her mind shrieked, why? How could she understand, though she could feel the pain; at seven it is difficult to accept explanations or understand unhappiness.

On reflection she supposed that on leaving Ceylon, a phase of her life was over and from then on things took on a different aspect. The memories that she had were no longer particularly fragmented, but seemed to link up. Time still did not enter into any of her activities or memories, but they seemed not only to be clearer but to be relevant to her existence.

Even on the voyage home there were incidents that she recalled which she considered relevant then. One was a dismal failure; the attempt to exert her own will-power over the very unnatural movement of the ship one day, by appearing in the dining-room for breakfast. The other was a lesson never quite forgotten. There was the race; crowds watching; hers the only head left, trying vainly to grasp a green apple so as to move on to the next obstacle; angry tears – disappointed voices impressing the need never to be a bad loser – shame – lesson learnt.

An Intoxicating Smell

My ambition, since I was not old enough to go to school, was to run away and join the circus. I would become a great performer of the big top. The swing was my servant and I its King and I prided myself that my will was the greater. I would spend my summer mornings performing death-defying tricks upon my throne, becoming increasingly professional. Each time the swing would come and catch me but a second before the skull touched the floor. One day, I decided that it was time that my hands should leave the safety of the chains. It was precisely at that moment that the swing decided to cast off its yoke of servitude throwing me into the outstretched hands of the rambling rose.

I remember the sharp entry of the thorns into the flesh and the sweet, intoxicating smell of the roses which appeared to lull the senses. A dull but distant scream rent the air, leaving the throat dry, the mind at peace and emotion taking over reason. I remember seeing a small animal fighting to get out of the arms of a not too friendly plant, and then rejoining the animal after it had been extracted from it.

The Giant Gasometers

Near my home there was a collection of overgrown fields and woods which I always played in. My friends and I called it the jungle because it seemed so big. Once you were in it you could be and do whatever you wanted. Whenever I stalked through the long grass of my territory I always felt a deep inner fear and respect for three giant gasometers which seemed to dominate the jungle. They were very fascinating but because of my deep inner fear I was scared to go near them. I can remember this fear very vividly and because of it the jungle provided me with many more dimensions to explore and play with. I think my friends also had this fear because none of them would go near the gasometers either. On one of the many occasions we played in the jungle I managed to get involved in a wager. If I went over and touched one of the gasometers I would get a bag of sweets. It seemed such a good offer that I started out without much thought walking across the fields. As I got further away from my friends and near the metal giants I began to weaken. I looked back to see if there was a way out but my friends just gazed at my progress, not knowing that I felt sick inside. There was no turning back because my friends would brand me a coward. I soon arrived at the base of the gasometer and looked up at it. It looked even worse now! The paint smelt funny and looked slimey. The time must have passed very slowly because I felt I had been there hours before I plucked up enough courage to touch it. I stretched out my hand with my fingers reaching over as far as they would go. Suddenly my fingers touched the cold metal and I instantly threw myself to the ground and waited for something to happen. Nothing happened! I felt so pleased! Now I could obtain my prize! I rushed back to my advancing friends. I had conquered the gasometers.

The Field

That field was heaven for me – the close, warm, smell of the grass and ferns in the summer – the cold, icy glitter of the frost on the leaves and grass in the winter. How many hours of my childhood that I spent in that garden of adventure, I will never be able to count. The thought that the people who read this passage do not know the holes and the trees and the brook and the paths and the mud – and the grassiness of it all – disappoints me and yet, in a way enlightens me because it was *my* secret, *my* life of adventure upon which no one can trespass except perhaps my sister and friend who accompanied me in my adventures. I yearn to be able to slide and bump down the winding slope of the field upon a greeny, tattered piece of cardboard which shone with the dye of the grass and which always eventually wore itself out on the land of that field which was mine! To see the brook which left many a gallon of water absorbed in my clothes on frequent occasions! 'Don't go near the brook today', my mother would warn me. How on earth could I manage to dry my clothes before tea-time?

Between the ages of six and ten I lived in this field in every spare hour I had. Apart from the dominant greenness and sweet smell of the grass, the most vivid event which hangs on my memory is Bonfire Night. Then, perhaps, my heart sank a little because my field was being crucified, burnt to a smouldering blackness, but I failed to remain in sad thoughts for long, for the exciting crackle and smoky sky alerted my sense of adventure. Stand too close and your cheeks burn fiercely, stand too far away and the cold wind pesters you in the cracks of your clothes. The smell of the fire and grass lingers with you for hours and hours afterwards and you hang onto the fading odour of branches and fire.

It is impossible to remember the field without recalling the friendliness, love and loyalty of one particular animal – a dog, Edward. He was a loyal subject and true friend, and this started within me the love of dogs and the belief in their love for mankind which I still possess today. I felt *then* and feel *now* that he would have followed me to the end of the earth. He was not my dog, but belonged to a neighbour and yet he spent most of his time accompanying my sister, her friend and myself on the adventures and my stories of our lives. He has died but cannot be forgotten – he was in no way a handsome show-dog but possessed the qualities which impressed me a great deal more.

From ten years of age onwards the field did not occupy my life in so great a force. In fact, I lived as if it did not exist at all, that is until my sister and myself were presented with a dog of our own – I was about fourteen and my sister sixteen. That dog was *my* life. The first time I saw her she appeared as a bounding white, fluffy ball with sparkling eyes. As soon as she saw both of us she attached herself completely to us and loved us from that moment. I touched her, smoothing her soft fur, attracted as a baby is to the hair of an adult. Was she really ours? Did she belong to us? Something living, breathing, moving of our own? The whole family adored her and gave her all the attention and love in their power. At the time of this loveable animal, we had in the house also, two cats. Of course they were astounded and disgusted at her presence and lived away from the house for at least two weeks but gradually learnt of the gentleness and almost human characteristics of the dog and finally accepted her into the family circle.

It was in the first two or three years of my friendship with the dog that the field was reborn into my life. Yes, again, I smelt the warm and yet fresh springiness of the grass. I came in contact yet again with the towering trees which I had conquered many a time. However, now I saw it in a different way: I usually seated myself on one particular rock at the top of the field and stared into the natural growth around, my dog at my side, of course. She seemed to share the greatness of this small field – I seemed to share my world with her. After a while I would feel a sense of triumph and excitement and run madly around the field with the dog barking at my heels. We always returned home exhausted after such an afternoon.

It was a wonderful time when I could come in contact with nature and its mysteries. I feel it was the only time when I was truly honest with myself and truly happy. My dog has died, and her death came as a fierce blow. For a while I hated nature and its clawing talons which had dragged my partner from me. But I gradually began to realize that she had become a part of the nature which we had both observed as outsiders – she was now inside, in the breath around me, in the trees, the grass, the wind and the land – she was still mine.

Formative Experiences

I remember little of my early childhood save that I was happy. Things and places seem better remembered than people who merely appeared and disappeared round the periphery of it all. My mother, of course, was always there, taken for granted. Only when she went away did I notice a gap in my life.

We lived next to a Church of England convent, and the nuns exerted a strong influence on my childhood. They were always there; I played in their gardens, they were my babysitters. I went to their Chapel; Sext, None, Vespers and the other daily services were familiar; and the Lighting of the New Fire, Midnight Mass and the Great Festivals marked the passage of time. I was very fond of the nuns I knew well, though there were others that frightened me. Sister Monica sometimes went to sleep when she played with me in the garden. This frail, saintly old lady was a diabetic. All the older nuns kissed me far too much for my liking and I dreaded being taken to the infirmary to visit the delicate old creatures, propped high on pillows, quavering in their white veils. It's strange that I never realised that nuns were women until I was about eleven years of age.

Old age and sickness were as much a part of my childhood as playing in the garden or making mud-pies in the bulldog's drinking bowl and damming the stream at the farm. My God-father's mother, who lived with us, had always been ill. I used to visit her room every evening before going to bed, stand on a stool at her bedside and watch transfixed as she took my hand in her own cold, wrinkled claw, and talked to me as if I were a hundred remembered children from years before. I might be Edith, Emily or Helen, all long dead, brought to life through my diminutive presence. I never knew when she died. I just stopped visiting her room and it was as though she had existed only in my imagination.

A little later – I must have been about six – my Godfather's old school friend, Bernard, came to live with us. He had recently had a stroke and came to us to convalesce. He stayed on as a paying guest until he too died. In the time he was with us he had several more strokes, and somehow I always knew when he was not well. He always seemed to become ill at lunchtime, and many times, in an agony of anxiety, I used to ask if I might not take my meal into the kitchen. The facial contortion and sickness which accompanied the strokes terrified me and I would stand cold, sweating and rooted to the spot until my mother's curt command broke the spell and sent me running to fetch the convent nurse. I ran – God how I ran – partly to get away, partly because I felt so helpless. All I could do was to fetch help, and that I did as fast as possible.

My school days at the convent kindergarten and junior school were uneventful, endured but not enjoyed, and then I was eleven and had passed the exam which was the door to grammar school, and I had my first real smell of success. . . .

About halfway along the road to adulthood I went through a very strange experience. A psychiatrist could probably explain it away in a few well-chosen words. It baffled me. At seven I had the sudden and world-shattering realisation that I was a human being, an individual, responsible to and for myself. Only I could think my thoughts, I was not a part of the adults around me. This revelation was at once exciting and terrifying. What would happen to me if my mother died? Should I have to go into a home? How does one arrange a funeral? Then it happened. I was barely eleven, and was dreading the transfer from junior to grammar school which was in a town eight miles away. My mother was taken suddenly and seriously ill and I watched her hunched and shivering form carried to the ambulance and taken away. For two weeks I filled her shoes as housekeeper – cooking, cleaning, shopping, washing, ironing as well as going to school. I hadn't time to worry about my mother, even visit her. Like my Godfather's mother, it was as though she had never been there. Something happened to me – I, with two friends from school already well practised in such things, took to shoplifting. I think that was the most unhappy period I ever lived through. I desperately wanted to be caught, and of course I was. The relief was incredible, and the Police were very understanding. I was back in focus, my mother was suddenly home and grammar school was fun. Retribution however was awful, though I knew it had to be to cleanse me of the terrible thing I had done. I had to go to confession and the pennance was that I should go to three of the people from whom I had stolen and ask their forgiveness. I got through it and the experience made me physically sick.

This was a turning point in my life. I was now aware not only of the fact that I was responsible, but also of what it means to betray oneself – a big step. I knew that my actions not only affected me, but those around me. I had seen the hurt in my Godfather's eyes, and that look I shall never forget. I came to recognise this, at the time terrible, experience as valuable and it helped me to formulate a kind of philosophy of life. Since that time my motto has been 'good or bad, put it all down as experience', and this has helped me a great deal.

The Power of Exams

And so my youth passed away to be re-born into adolescence. School obviously formed a major influence as might be expected. I hated almost all of it, I remained a generally mediocre pupil, rarely exalting, occasionally failing. Above all I loathed the community spirit of the place – I enjoyed being alone. The work was irritating, the importance attached to it, it seemed, excessive. I never felt the pressure of success/failure until the age of eleven. Prior to the eleven plus we were drilled and instructed in the manner of the test. Most emphasis was placed on the importance of the examination. However, of this event I fortunately remember little, apart from the fact that I felt slightly sick all day. Results, however, were a different matter. The pass or fail, the ticket to education or obscurity came by post. We all knew this as we sat in the classroom that day. A young student from the local College of Education was attempting to teach English. His class were very quiet but completely unresponsive. Then one of the children's mothers arrived waving the results above her head. Her equally overjoyed son ran from the classroom into her arms whilst the rest of us looked on through the window, each of us wishing to change places with that boy. And so the morning wore on, one dutiful parent after another arrived to bestow glad tidings until finally about ten had visited. This still left about three quarters of the class uninformed. The pressure and strain were almost audible. When the eleventh parent arrived one girl (said by the headmaster to show great potential, no less) began to cry. It was as if the teacher had given a positive command, the room erupted in availing forms bemoaning their fate. I watched in fascination at the scene set before me. The poor student was especially out of his depth – College had obviously not prepared him for this 'teaching situation'. So amazed was I that I actually forgot to cry but merely watched the antics of others. The intermittent sobs continued until dinner-time when the school received the results. I look back and regard it lamentable that the course for life should be set at such tender years. At the time, however, those results were my world.

Holbrook School

Holbrook is the name that stands out in my life. My memories of it are mixed, but no matter how hard I try to be grateful for the benefits it has given me, there still lurks a feeling that its effect has not been an entirely beneficial one. Holbrook is a village near Ipswich in Suffolk, or rather it is a boarding school, because the school comprises more than half of the inhabitants. The central tower of the Royal Hospital School is as impressive as its name, dominating the countryside for miles around, and I knew that once I had seen it I was part of the establishment again. Indeed, the whole school was an architectural marvel, overlooking the Stour estuary across to Essex, and it did credit to its historical and architectural counterpart at Greenwich, both schools being built by Sir Christopher Wren.

The seven hundred boys at this boarding school wear a naval rating's uniform, the only difference being that up to the fifth form all of them wear blue serge shorts. These proved to be very uncomfortable in winter because the coarseness of the material together with damp weather soon made one's legs very sore. The dye in these trousers also has a tendency to run causing a phenomena which must be unique to this school of having blue legs! But for all its disadvantages our uniform had its good aspects. There's a saying that all the nice girls like a sailor, and sure enough, whenever we were given sixth-form leave to go into Ipswich the attention we got was secretly welcomed by all of us, although it was thought soft to admit it.

As new boys, or new jacks as we were called, we were regarded as a lower form of life, with few privileges if any. In the mess we sat at the bottom of a long table, with twenty or thirty boys to a table. If any leftover food reached us we considered ourselves as having received a divine benefaction from the self-made gods at the top of the table. For this reason and others we all awaited the day when we too could hold this position of superiority. But like a lot of things, when we achieved our end it wasn't the paradise we expected. Duty rotas for looking after the younger boys proved to be as irksome to the badgeboys (all prefects were given the rank of either chief or petty officer) as it did to the boys being supervised.

Smartness and bearing was the ideal pressed upon us as new boys. Every night our shoes had to be polished, and polished well, or we went without supper. Not that this really mattered, because the same biscuits year in, year out, don't arouse much enthusiasm. It wasn't wise, however, to attract too much attention with these minor misdemeanors, for when the final crunch came and they were all considered and accumulated together, they didn't leave you with a leg to stand on. As time went on I unconsciously became an accomplished liar. I did not fully appreciate how deceitful I was becoming until one day in my fifth year when I was presented in front of the housemaster for drinking in a pub in Ipswich on a theatre visit. This cardinal sin would have lost me all my privileges, the most coveted being loss of study, petty officer's stripe, and worst of all, loss of face in front of my junior inferiors. I realised I had got myself into a truly hazardous situation, worsened by the fact that my chief accuser was another master, and that it was perhaps going to require more guile than I could muster to squirm out of it. But I managed it. Two perspiring hours of plaintive persuasion got me off the hook, together with my equally guilty brother and two other associates. When I left the housemaster's study I felt strangely exalted, and to my surprise I was even convinced of my innocence! Smartness to our masters was a matter of personal tidiness, but to us it was the ability to remain incognito, or even better, to be known as a responsible individual.

I liked to think, and still do, that these instances of deception helped me to be a better badgeboy in the two sixth-form years. When you were deceitful yourself, you could more often than not detect it in others. So when it was obvious that one of the younger boys was trying to lie his way out of trouble, it was not difficult to get the truth eventually. At the same time, I realised myself how degrading it had been for me to crawl out of trouble, and rather than resort to lying, tried thenceforth to avoid the question.

An Unexpected Event with New Words

The door bell rang and I stood by the sitting room door as my mother came along the hall and opened the front door. The man at the door saluted; they were all doing it today!

'Mrs Goodman? I wonder if I could have a few words with you?'

He came in removing his cap. 'Hello, you're Terry aren't you? A happy Christmas to you, young man.'

'Thank you, sir. A happy Christmas to you. I've got a train set.'

'My word, can I come and see it in a minute? I just want to talk to your mummy for a little while.'

'I'll wind it up ready,' I said.

I went back to the train and occupied myself while my mother and the air force man went into the dining room. My door was wide open and their door was only partially closed. For two or three minutes I heard only the sound of voices, mainly the man's. I was not attempting to overhear, being too concerned with arranging the train for our visitor, but after a short time I heard a louder sound. My mother said 'Oh! Oh!' twice, quite distinctly, and then I heard the unmistakable sound of crying.

My mother! Crying? I had never known such a thing. I had seen and heard adult women crying outside bomb-shattered houses as I walked to school, but grown-up tears in our house were unknown. That apparently nice air force man must be saying very unpleasant things to my mother. I must protect her, and stop him! I was carrying the tin railway station as I ran across the hall and into the dining room.

My mother was sitting at the table, still sobbing. In front of her was the air force man's briefcase and cap. He was standing by her chair, with one hand on her shoulder. They both looked up as I rather burst in, and my mother wiped her eyes and smiled. I ran up to her and, as the man stepped away a little she put her arms round me. I looked at her red eyes.

'What are you crying for, mummy?' Not waiting for an answer I said to the man, leaning round her, 'I'll tell grandpa you've been nasty to her! At the weekend when he comes home from London.'

'It's all right, dear,' said my mother. 'No one's been nasty to me. I was crying because I was happy and had rather a shock.'

This was most peculiar. I only cried when I was miserable or hurt. I laughed when I was happy. But my mother was continuing her explanation.

'This is Group Captain Lerwell. He's come from Uxbridge to tell us two rather wonderful pieces of news. Daddy's been awarded the D.F.C. and Uncle John has been found alive with other prisoners in Germany.'

'How can daddy be given something? He's dead . . . isn't he?'

'Yes dear, he is dead. But the award is posthumous, because of what he did just before he died.'

'What's posthumous?'

'It means realising how brave someone was after they have died,' said the group captain coming round to me and sitting down. 'There were five other men in your father's aeroplane and when it was shot down by the Germans they all escaped by jumping out with their parachutes. Some of those men have now arrived back in England, now that the war is over, and that's how we know what happened. Your father kept the plane flying long enough for them all to bale out, but too long to get out himself. This is the citation.' He handed me a piece of paper he had been holding.

I looked at it. It was rather like a letter because it had Buckingham Palace where the address should be, and a date, but it didn't say 'Dear anybody' like a proper letter. It had a lot of words I didn't understand, 'valour; selfless; well-beloved; hostilities' and at the bottom there was no 'love from anybody', or kisses, just a name, an odd name really.

'Who's George R.I.?' I asked.

'It's the King,' said my mother. 'I have to go to Buckingham Palace next month instead of Daddy, as he can't be there.' She was almost crying again now, but smiling as well. A most peculiar combination I thought.

'And there's our other wonderful piece of news,' she went on. 'We had thought Uncle John was dead, too, as we hadn't heard from him for a year. But his name is on a list of prisoners of war which has just arrived from the Americans in Germany. He's in one of their hospitals, and will be home in a few weeks.'

This was another man like my father, one of whom I had heard much spoken in the family, but could not remember. His photograph was on the sitting room mantelpiece opposite my father's. For as long as I could remember they had smiled down from either side of the clock. He was my mother's brother, not my father's, but they had always looked rather similar to me with their identical caps and uniforms and the wings on their jackets. The writing was the same on the frames as well; *Per Ardua Ad Astra*. That was a piece of Latin I knew long before I went to school.

I do not think I recall my mother going to Buckingham Palace as I was not involved in it. For the purpose of writing these recollections I asked her to describe the day from my point of view, but it failed to stir any memories.

Grammar School Failure

I will concentrate on the secondary-school experience . . . It must be appreciated that this was 1959. Ours was a semi-rural school and the majority of the children there, nearly all girls, were not at all interested in going to a secondary-grammar or even technical school. I was not at all concerned myself and had never given much thought to the future. My father, essentially a self-made man, was convinced of the value of education as long as it was not taken too seriously and so it was decided that I should be 'put down' for the grammar school and that I should attempt some extra work at home.

The suggestion was not favourably received and long negotiations were commenced before a compromise of two hours a day twice a week was arrived at. The football team was incredulous.

'Yer going to work instead of playing footer? Yer must be nuts.' And I could not really argue with them. Luckily I had an ally in my best friend Hoppy, whose father was also involved in the devious 'Red-Dragon' plot, and it was agreed that we would work together in my bedroom and have a game of blow-football, always Leeds v. Manchester, afterwards.

The 'scholarship' results were announced in rather an unreal way. The whole school was assembled and the names of the successful were read out. I had passed and was allowed to run home and tell my parents and collect my bribe money. Hoppy had failed and had to remain behind, crying dejectedly.

The summer holidays came and things continued much as usual. It was cricket nearly every day. Can you imagine that? Cricket, cricket, cricket. We all thought, ate and slept cricket for weeks on end. Twice in the pond and you're out, hitting the hedge counts as four, and of course I had a new cricket bat bought with my 'bribe' money. Hoppy too had a new bat, identical to mine, a sort of consolation prize I suppose.

As the holidays drew to a close, my parents' thoughts, at least, were drawn to my new school and we had a shopping expedition to town to buy the uniform. I can remember standing in front of a mirror feeling very pleased with myself. I was made aware that I would have a considerable advantage over the majority of the other first-years by the fact of my already having a brother established at school.

The first day duly arrived. I walked proudly with my brother to the school bus and made for some empty seats at the back to receive my first rude awakening from my supposed ally.

'Oh, you can't sit there, our kid, it's reserved for seniors.' I retired red-faced to the front to be confronted with many new faces, none of which spoke on the forty-minute journey to school. The bus was very crowded and we had to stand all the way.

We eventually arrived and emerged dishevelled from the coach into an immense quadrangle surrounded by huge red-brick buildings. We had hardly time to take in any fresh air before we were herded into lines, alphabetical order. I placed myself at the front amongst the 'B's', that is the Brians, and was consequently sent to the wrong classroom for registration.

'Name, boy.'

'Brian.'

'Surname?'

'Willet.'

'You should be in B2. Go there at once.'

By the time I found B2 they were in the middle of copying down the form timetable. I did not understand what a timetable was and copied it imperfectly and in a total daze.

We were then quizzed as to what we had already accomplished at primary school.

'Who knows any French?'

Scores of arms shot into the air.

'Geometry or Algebra?'

More arms, but again, not mine. I was beginning to feel very inferior.

Break came – but where was my brother? At primary school he was always by my side or at least easily findable, but now he was nowhere to be seen. There were two more confused periods and then lunch time and my first experience of school meals. The canteen was over-full and we had to carry our plates of gruel to the cadet-hut about a hundred yards away. I could eat very little of my meal and had to carry it back to the canteen through the 'quad', now swarming with boys who did their best to make me drop the lot.

And so it went on. I was near to tears throughout the day. The masters seemed so impersonal in their black gowns. The buildings were large and dismal. The walls were plain and grim in stark contrast to the amateur-painting-covered walls of our primary school. I could not wait to get home and broke into tears. We were not given any homework in the first week, only innumerable tatty books which we had to back with brown paper.

I found the lessons very difficult. The whole system was totally new to me. 'If you can't understand anything ask me after the lesson or come to the staffroom' was all very well, but I was extremely diffident at that age, the masters in their flowing gowns seeming as unapproachable as the gods. Once when I found a piece of maths homework totally unfathomable I girded my loins and sought out the maths master, 'Killer Kelsey', in the staff-room. The door was open; 'Killer' was in a group of teachers in the centre of the room with his back to the door. I knocked softly. The games master popped his head around the door.

'Well, Willet, what is it?'

'Please may I see Mr Kelsey, sir?'

'Can't you see he's busy? Go away.'

Needless to say it was my last trip to the staffroom and meant another 'See me' in my maths exercise book and a reprimand without an explanation.

At first I really did try with the homework and spent much more than the recommended norm of two hours. Besides being unable to grasp what was being said, I was also a terrible writer. We had not progressed to using fountain pens at primary school until about the last six months and my written work was more than usually 'blotchy'.

The homework incidents in the first term clearly stand out in my memory. In History we were studying ancient Greece and were given the task for homework of tracing an outline of the country from our Atlas into our exercise book. My first attempt resulted in the usual unrecognisable mess but I was struck by a remarkable brainwave. I had an old Atlas of my own and removed the Greek map from it, carefully cut round the edges, and glued the resulting figure into my book on top of the original outline.

I then 'improved' the whole thing, shading the 'sea' blue, carefully printing the title and handed in the finished totality with some pride, the next day. My originality was not appreciated: the page was torn from the book, I was beaten before the class for insolence and told to do it 'properly' by the next morning.

There was a similar incident in a Geography lesson where again I expended considerable time on 'equinoxes' and 'solstices' and was reduced to tears by red crossings out and the comment that it was the 'scruffiest thing seen in twenty years of teaching'. Before the end of the first term, I had stopped doing homework almost entirely. I discovered that I could easily do the required minimum on the school bus in the morning, a forty-minute ride, which of course did not improve my handwriting.

It was at the end of October that the gang started to re-form, drawn together by common excursions to the woods to collect material for the coming bonfire night. Membership was confined essentially to one or two streets and not as previously to the 'top class' of the primary school. Hoppy was very rarely seen now. He had called twice during the early days of term only to be told that I was doing homework by my parents, and had left on both occasions without seeing me.

Soon my thoughts were centred entirely on the gang. I lived for weekends, when we would play non-stop football and in the dark evenings would light bonfires and 'cook' turnips and sausages and potatoes. I stopped worrying about school. My clearest memories of this period are out-of-school ones, the fishing trips, the apple scrumping, the secret sex initiation ceremonies in Ingram's barn.

I found I could get away with doing very little at school. Stock excuses like 'I left my book on the bus, sir', or 'I forgot the question' were regularly used and there was a general lassitude amongst the staff allowing me, more often than not, to avoid doing the work altogether.

The Christmas examinations came and I finished 25th out of a class of 27. I was not unduly worried. My real interests were in football tables, not form positional tables. I remember once being with a number of the real rogues of the school, the '4-B-ites'. They asked me whether I was at all like my brother.

'What position did you come in the Christmas exams?'

'Twenty-fifth.'

'Ah, it's okay, chaps, he's one of us.'

I blushed with pride at being included in that select band.

And so it went on . . .

My Teachers

Assembly was in the first year or two at school a rather awe-inspiring procedure because I had tremendous respect for my first headmistress. It was also uncomfortable however, as we had to sit on the floor and were so cramped that we rose and sank down together in a mass each dragging the others with her. Subsequently Assembly was a bore and eventually an ordeal when I played the hymn on the piano and showed off with a suitably dignified performance of Handel's *Largo* or *Song Without Words*.

A new headmistress came to the school after I had been there for three years. She was a complete contrast to her predecessor and no one ever liked or respected her. This change in head-mistresses came at a crucial time for me as it was when I really began to question authority and my total lack of respect for my headmistress annoyed and upset me – partly, in fact, because I couldn't understand how the teachers whom I liked and admired could bear her stupidity.

There were three teachers whom I respected greatly and was very fond of. I can remember a particular nail varnish that one of these, who was an English teacher, wore. It was a very dark pearly red and I can remember her fingers with their long, shaped nails very thickly coated in this varnish, holding her poetry book upright before her; and I can see her oddly shaped mouth with lipstick matching her nail varnish just above the top of the book. There was something slightly decadent about her though she was a warm and elegant person.

Another of the three was also an English teacher. She was a sad woman of about twenty-eight. Her hair was untidy and her lipstick smudged and she always wore the same few dresses. Everyone always wondered why. She taught in a friendly way which my form always appreciated, yet I remember that some of the other girls hated her. She was, on the whole, the most popular teacher in the school. She had evidently a line which she had drawn between herself and most of the girls, which some of them came too close to sometimes I think. She was one of the most special people in my life for six years and I always felt that there was a bond between us. She told my parents when I was fourteen that she identified herself with me – that she saw in me herself at my age, and that she knew instinctively what my reactions would be. I loved her for that. During my last years at school she used to communicate with me a great deal by looks and used sometimes to startle me by supplying an answer to something I was thinking about. It helped me to know that someone understood my sadness. I was very sad in my last year at school. My disillusionment was increasing all the time – not just with school and with authority, but with everything in my life. I remember the autumn of that year and how, for the first time, it really hurt me. Keats bothered me a great deal because I was desperate to find a Truth – a constant – a reality – at a time when life seemed to consist of layers of pretence and fabrication.

I wished very much that I did not need to go to school and act daily a part which I felt was very much based upon and involved in pretence. Everything about the mood of that last year in school suggests decay when I think back to it, and I can smell the grime of the floorboards and the darkness of the old house in which the upper sixth worked, including, especially, that of a room whose window was more or less obscured by a thick creeper. The light there was always strange as it filtered in through the leaves, and I can remember sitting in it translating French Romantic poetry in a spirit of morbid exhilaration.

Teachers' clothes always made an impression on me and on what they taught me. One had hair that was often dirty and she wore pastel mohair jumpers and summer dresses with wide sashes and enormous skirts. Her shoes had small boring bows on the toes.

Another wore bright, tight-fitting jersey dresses and green, red and orange shoes. She was disliked by many of the staff partly, she used to tell me, because she had been married twice and they were jealous. She gave me piano lessons in the school lunch hours and told me the staffroom scandal which I revelled in.

Another teacher wore nothing but purple because she said it was the royal colour of the Caesars. She had an amazing obsession for Julius Caesar, for Charles Dickens and for 'culture'. I hated her for her rudeness. She taught Latin and I hated it. I have met few people more insulting than she was yet she worked hard and took us on a great many cultural visits on Saturdays. Those days had a most distinct smell of guide books and sandwiches mixed together. They were days of studied earnestness (something I was very good at) yet real pleasure too, but they always ended in a quiz.

I worked hard but this was mainly through fear. I lived in dread of punishment or correction, which I would have found extremely hard to take. I was always very aware of the injustices of school life and I resented being part of it. I see myself working, talking, moving around, in a kind of bubble of sensitivity. I was always pleased about my awareness and fastidiousness yet I also disliked the latter for the constraints it placed upon me. I built up a character – an image – which required protection from crudeness and vulgarity and which my friends believed in. Even with them I led a conflicting existence and could not always really relax. I conditioned myself to outwardly reject behaviour which I didn't feel was in character with me.

I always despised teachers who seemed to base their opinions of people on their degree of talkativeness in lessons – on the number of questions they answered. It was very rare for me not to know an answer to a question but I hardly ever volunteered it and refused to co-operate with the teachers. I had a high opinion of my own sensitivity and intelligence and felt that it was up to the teachers to ascertain this. Some, in fact, did. The dread of answering questions and, at the same time, of not answering, has never left me. If I could ever bring myself to volunteer an answer in class I always had a feeling of tremendous relief yet always thought afterwards about what I had said, wondering how stupid or unnecessary it had sounded. This still happens, however well I understand a topic under discussion. I still have the feeling of cold suffocation which I felt at school when I am asked a question.

I always despised my lack of co-operation at school. I am sure that it was a result of wishing to be considered as an individual and also as a result of moving from Monmouthshire at the age of twelve – from an area where I had always been top, in my Junior School and in my first grammar school, to a school of high academic standard where at least thirty people of my age were just as bright as I.

I was very sorry indeed to be forced to give up geography, chemistry and art, especially art, at the age of fourteen. I remember struggling vainly to have my timetable arranged so that I could do art. My art teacher told my parents even before this occurred that as I was one of the 'poor little A's' I should not be allowed to continue with her subject.

I failed Maths and have never really been able to forget this fact. I could never do Maths. I had never done Geometry in my other schools and I never caught up despite extra coaching.

I remember my headmistress saying in Assembly one day that anyone who passed the 11-plus should be ashamed not to pass 'O'-level Maths, English and French. It annoyed me, though I'm sure that she was quite justified in saying that.

I always regarded her as a particularly insensitive person. I remember after she had been at the school for a term we gave her a travelling rug for Christmas. After the presentation she said that she already had one but she was sure that her son who had just got married would find ours useful. Her eyes were expressionless and cold and she usually wore a grey suit and sensible shoes.

In my school the chosen Few, which included me, took some 'O' levels and certain 'A' levels a year in advance of the others. We were also privileged to take our exams under the London Board whereas those deemed less intelligent had life made easy by being given Oxford Board exams. I remember the particularly ludicrous arrangement whereby I began courses in 'O'- and 'A'-level English Literature at the same time. It irritated and confused me to have to change from Betjeman's *Greenway* to John Donne's sonnets, or from character studies of *Northanger Abbey* to discussions on Fielding's Irony at the ringing of a bell for lesson changes.

Another example of the ludicrousness of my education was doing 'O'-level German in two years with one lesson per week and actually being sent into a German oral exam without ever having spoken German to my teacher who was always more interested in talking in English about her cats.

Travelling to and from school was always a nightmare as I used London transport buses which are usually non-existent at the most crucial times. I remember the particularly degrading struggles that took place between schoolchildren and shoppers in an effort to get home in the afternoon. Strangely enough the fact that we were issued with school travelling passes suggested to the more ignorant adults that we had less right to travel than they did and I can remember angry shouts of 'Get all the brown kids off the bus' (our uniform was brown) from certain women to the bus conductor.

That is probably why this part of London does not seem to me to be a place to stay in now, but a place to escape from whenever I go there, which is rarely. Whenever I travel along the road past the school I feel the choking suffocation of swaying buses filled with cigarette smoke and rain-wet clothes and almost automatically still think with a feeling of sickness that the horror of Double Games or a Latin lesson awaits me at the end of my journey.

The Death of My Mother

She had given me life and now they said she was dead. It was strange to be standing there so near to her and yet so far. I felt cheated that I couldn't remember her as she must have been. They said they couldn't understand why she was ill, when she looked so healthy. But I suppose it's lucky in a way that I was too young to see and remember. I remember how unusual it felt on that day, to be part of the congregation instead of singing my heart out in the choirstalls. I remember too gazing up towards the great east window thinking it was ironic to hear the cloaked priest giving a sermon about someone he had never known. I remember vividly watching my father's fingers attempt to find the correct page of the hymn-book. Somehow he could just not manage it and my brother had to help him. It was one of those rare occasions when I felt a great affinity, a sense of oneness with my father.

They had cut the grass in the churchyard and the morning rain made it stick to my newly polished shoes. Everyone stood back solemn faced in the weak October sunshine.

I remember when we all gathered together afterwards, one of my relations saying 'it's a pity we only meet at weddings or funerals'.

IV From the Author's Autobiography

The Vocation
An Autobiographical Story

I

At the age of eleven I decided I had a vocation. I decided I had been called by God to return our sad and desiccated humanity to its original state of joy and unity. Where had my sudden sense of mission come from? At the time I would have thought – though never dared to have said – that it was the bright edge of God's will thrusting itself into my life. And yet, looking back, my desire to be a priest had not arrived in any dramatic form, had not issued from the strange world of dreams nor burst into my mind when I knelt expectantly before Our Lady's candlelit statue. In fact, one evening, after Benediction, Father Rye had suggested it to me. Father Rye had said that to be a priest was the highest calling, the greatest blessing and had given me a dozen pamphlets to read. The pamphlets were about startling and unexpected vocations; they made me want to rise flame-like towards the distant and ineffable joys of heaven. And so I began to long for martyrdom and the sanctity which, a hundred years after my earthly torments, the church would declare mine.

If my unexpected passion for the priesthood had been tolerated but not indulged it would, no doubt, have slowly crumbled and fallen away or under the moulding of later interests been turned into a smoother and rounder shape. As it happened my eleven-year-old fantasy was not left alone. The news of an early vocation threw my mother into a sustained state of elation. Her son – a priest? The thought pierced her heart with a sharp happiness. There was no greater gift she could make! No greater sacrifice! Every night she knelt at the side of her bed and prayed for the strength to let her son go, to let him become God's man.

149

My father said very little. He never spoke easily about his deepest feelings. But I could see he was unhappy. His opposition expressed itself in fierce gusts of irritability which swept round us whenever my vocation was mentioned. His disapproval intensified my determination to follow the path I felt divinely revealed to me. I even saw his anger as a sign. Hadn't Christ Himself said he had come to bring spiritual war and discord, to set child against parent, truth against falsity? What vocation could exist without sorrow and conflict? Without the son pitted against the father? And as son, I was determined to win. I would become a priest. I would moisten and cast seeds in the parched and dying earth. I would show my father. I was right. He was wrong.

In the dark winter evenings my mother began filling in entrance forms to all the main junior seminaries. Later I was interviewed at many – but I continually failed to pass the necessary exams. I was angry at the time not so much because I failed to pass but more because I couldn't see what trivial exams had to do with divine vocations. In the pamphlets it had talked about being simple, stubborn, humble, persistent, but never about being intelligent. Would Saint Francis of Assissi, so quick to discard the wealthy trappings of his life, have passed an open examination? I doubted it. Then why should I feel daunted by failing? I had no intention of giving up – merely because I was stupid.

One morning a letter came from Saint Paul's Seminary. I remember the day vividly. And now, twenty years later, I recall its small details. I feel if I turn the simple events of that day over long enough, if I scrutinise them carefully, if I slowly piece them together, I may be able to arrive at a true understanding of my vocation.

II

It must have been January or February when the letter arrived for I remember it was dark outside the kitchen window as we were eating our breakfast under the heavy yellow glow of the gaslight. I was sitting between my elder brother, Martin, and my father. Martin, immune to my mother's patter about missing the school-bus, was anxiously flicking over the pages of some school book – Latin, I think it was. My father was crouching over the tiny kitchen table, morosely jabbing at the thin rasher of bacon on his plate. My mother was busily running between us, now holding out a clean knife, now a cup of tea, now the sugar.

Suddenly I noticed the postman's hand pushing two letters through the open window and guiding them through the layers of white lace curtains which protected us from the outside world. I ran to collect them.

One of the letters was familiar to me, it was thick, square and without a proper stamp. The other was long and thin and unfamiliar. Suddenly my father plucked the squarish one from my hands.

He felt the letter carefully between his thumb and his fingers, sighed, and took it over to his private shelf above the boiler.

'Any luck?' said my mother.

'Not bloody likely!'

'How can you tell?' said Martin still looking down at his Latin verbs.

'Me?' said my father, 'I could feel a cheque through a stack of newspapers.'

'I don't know how,' said my mother.

'It's what's called extra-sensory perception.'

'Well,' said my mother, 'they don't give you much chance to practise it, do they?'

'The buggers don't give you a chance.' – My mother's comment had been too close to the truth for my father to be amused – 'Them in the Pools don't write out cheques for poor bleeders like me. That they don't.'

My mother made no reply. But I sensed her spinning away into her own world. She always recoiled from any intensity of feeling in my father. And she particularly loathed what she called his 'coarse language'.

My father sighed, heavily. Then as if to express his contempt for the powers that be – and, perhaps, also, to prickle my mother – he sucked his cheeks together and sent out a thick lump of phlegm into the kitchen sink.

'You dirty pig!' shouted my mother. She thrust back her head in disgust.

But father took no notice. And seemed to quickly sink back into his previous state of slumber. He sat down. He pushed the bacon to one side of his plate and began soaking up the grease with a thick wad of bread.

I now looked more closely at the other letter. The envelope was glossy brown and was addressed in type (though then I didn't know what type was) to Mr and Mrs Rowland. I sensed its importance and instinctively handed it to my mother.

Without a word my mother selected a knife from the draining board and slit open the envelope. The letter was neatly folded and, as my mother opened it, I noticed at the top of the page a coat of arms or a badge which had large upright letters on either side of it.

As she read, Martin and I waited apprehensively.

At last my mother spoke.

'They've taken you!' she said. 'At Saint Paul's. The seminary. They've given you a place. To start next term. The letter is from the rector.'

For a second I was aware of my mother's lips hovering near my cheeks but she was too excited to kiss me. Tears were forming in the corners of her eyes. And the words came cascading from her mouth.

'A priest! A priest! God is good and kind. He's heard my prayers. My novenas. Nothing has been in vain. I knew you could pass those exams with God's help. I knew it.'

I felt strangely elated too. I laughed and said –

'After so many weeks and months I never thought –'

Then Martin, still holding his book, put his arm round my neck. 'Well done,' he said. 'Well done.'

For one moment the three of us were entwined together, happy and all talking at once. But our union was abruptly ended.

'What's all this about?' said my father.

'A priest!' chanted my mother. 'A priest!'

'A priest?' said my father. 'Are you out of your mind, woman?'

'Read the letter then.'

My mother held out the letter. I had never seen her so confident – so imperial in her gestures.

'I don't need to read the letter,' said my father. 'I understand that much. I know you can just about manage to read a letter.'

I disentangled myself from my mother's arms. I felt myself shrinking from her affection. I wanted to stand alone before my father. I wanted *his* appreciation. Didn't he realise I had a vocation? That I, his son, had been called by God?

But my mother's feelings were too strong to be hurt by my father's sarcasm.

'You ought to be proud,' she said. 'Think what your father had to do all his life. What did he ever provide for your mother? No money. And no respect either.'

'My father used his hands.'

'And where did it get him?'

'His work *was* work. And it was good enough for him.'

'That's because he had no ambition.'

'That's as may be.'

'Well,' said my mother, 'your sons will use their minds. And you can be sure they will be respected for it. People will look up to them.'

I looked at my mother, startled. I had no idea what she was talking about. What had my vocation to do with my mind? I didn't want to study like Martin at the Grammar School. I hated books. I wanted to be a saint and convert the world. I wanted to be a martyr lovingly holding out a crucifix to those who burnt me. What had that to do with using my mind?

'Look,' said my father, suddenly clenching his fists and rolling them on the table, 'I'm not talking about my father. Poor bugger. He sweated for every penny he got. But leave him out of it. And leave me out of it too. I know I'm not respected. I'm nobody. Nothing at all. Never will be. But that don't matter either. What I ask is this. One question. How old is a bloke before – before he's turned into a priest?'

'You mean before he's ordained?' I said, stepping towards my father. I felt pleased that at last the discussion had come back to my vocation.

'If that's what you call it – very well,' said my father.

'Twenty-four,' I said – for Father Rye had told us this in his last catechism class.

'You can shut up!' said my father with unexpected fierceness.

'But –' I said.

'Don't you dare speak to John like that,' said my mother.

Suddenly my father stopped rolling his fists on the table and clutching a fork held it straight out towards my mother.

'It's *you* I'm talking to,' he said.

'For the fear of God put that fork down,' said my mother, tugging at my blazer and pulling me out of my father's reach.

'I'll put it down as soon as you answer!' said my father, 'and not before.'

'What John says is the truth,' said my mother. Then, appeasingly, 'A man has to be twenty-four before he can be ordained.'

'Well then' – my father now jerked the fork away from my mother's face and began cleaning his nails with its prongs – 'he's far from being a priest, isn't he? Far from it. He's only a kid.

A.E.—6

Isn't he? A little kid. Look at his knees! They're as rough as cheese graters from shinning up trees and skidding over.'

I looked down at my knees. I felt small. And ashamed of it.

My mother glanced at my knees as well. She knew all about them. She was always sticking plasters over them. But she could also see into the future, she could see a time when they would be covered by grey flannel and flashing out from the dim uncertainty of the future she could see them kneeling before the bishop on the day of ordination. At the back of the church, inconspicuous but happy, she could see herself. And by her side she could see Martin, a doctor, in a discreet suit and donning an exquisite carnation. Yes – my knees were rough and the colour of ripe plum juice, but what did it matter? How could such an ephemeral detail hold back her flood of dreams? Or prevent God's will?

'Can't you see,' said my father, 'he might just as well want to be a sea captain or an all-in wrestler. Like other boys.'

'Like other boys!' sneered my mother.

'Yes,' said my father, 'like other boys.'

Father said no more. He seemed content. What he had said was as obvious to him as the dark stain of Brylcream round the edge of his cap, as clear as the yellow stain of nicotine which spread down his first two fingers. He assumed, I think, that he had pulled down to earth the dizzy heights of my vocation.

He stood up, looked critically at the three of us, took his oil-smeared overalls from the hook on his private shelf, and left the room.

We waited while he dragged his overalls on outside in the porch – a habit my mother had inculcated. Nor did we speak or move till we heard his footsteps disappear down the street outside.

'Never mind,' said my mother, soothingly, 'it's a great blessing. If you hurry down to church you'll be able to get the last part of Mass and thank God for what he has made known.'

I pulled my green school cap out of the table drawer. I bent down and pulled up my socks, turning them neatly over so that the yellow lines at the top would show.

'And don't worry what your father said. He'll come round in the end. He'll see that it is God's will.'

I stood on the chair and combed my hair in the mirror.

'Oh, and don't forget to tell Father Rye about the letter. He'll be so excited.'

'Righto,' I said, as I ran out of the kitchen, through the porch, to get my brother's racing bike from the shed.

I couldn't wait to be in church.

I must thank God.

I must make new resolutions. Renew my act of dedication.

And I must not forget to pray for my father.

III

It was still dark as I began to run with the bike, putting my left foot on the pedal and trying to swing the right leg over the top of the saddle. I had always found it difficult to hoist my leg over the saddle. Sometimes I just didn't stretch that far. At other times the bike tipped menacingly away from me until it crashed noisily on the road with me sprawled across it and the back wheel spinning round and round. Still I insisted on riding it whenever I could because it was a racing bike. And it was my brother's. And my brother was at Grammar School.

This dark morning I mounted the bike on my second attempt and with my toes – for my heels never reached the pedals – drove the wheels round for all I was worth. I could hear the back wheel rubbing and whirring against the dynamo and I could see the light in front of me coming stronger and stronger. I took the short cut. Down the first lane. Across the common. Over the stream. And up past the red-brick council school. At each corner, I skidded, rang my bell and, making an arch with my legs, aimed for any puddles I could see.

Three minutes later I was gliding through the church gates trying to swing my right leg back over the saddle and at the same time trying to jerk the bike to a halt – for the brake blocks had long been rubbed down to the metal.

I stepped quietly into the church porch. I dabbed my fingers into the holy water font and making an abbreviated sign of the cross, entered by the main altar. The white marble was bare and in deep gloom. Above it, the sanctuary lamp in an ornate silver chamber, flickered, a violet blue. I genuflected and walked down the side aisle to the small side chapel where I could hear the murmur of the Mass drifting across the fathomless deeps of prayer.

I loved the tiny chapel as much as I hated the high altar which was used on Sundays and throughout the summer months.

Hearing Mass at the high altar was like eating a prescribed meal in a railway cafeteria whereas in the chapel it was like sharing an unexpected tea round the fire. At the main altar the secret words of the Mass were constantly lost in the exterior noises – the door banging, the chairs scraping, coins dropping. But in the chapel it was different: there, the holy words rippled and eddied round you, they caressed you, and with an infinite delicacy of movement beckoned you towards the unknown. Also in the chapel there stood the high silver stand in which Our Lady of Walsingham candles blazed in uneven circles of light. And the dense fumes of burning wax was everywhere.

I slipped through the purple curtain which divided the chapel from the side aisle and kneeling down at the first bench, closed my eyes and prayed. I thanked God for granting me a vocation. I told him I wanted to be a saint. That I wanted to convert the world rather than go to the Grammar School. That I would do un-flinchingly anything he wished of me. That I would endure all forms of torture. That I would be crucified upside down. Or if God preferred it, burnt at the stake. No pain or tortures inflicted by heathens would ever get me to disown the true religion.

I prayed too for my poor father. I asked God to help him to understand my vocation and to grant him greater faith.

And as I prayed my spirit seemed to drift out of my small body and float towards the silent and shimmering waters of eternity.

At the end of Mass I waited as the altar boy blew out the candles on either side of the small golden tabernacle and folded the starched white communion cloths. Then I genuflected and passing by the side of the altar entered the sacristy. There already out of his golden vestments and in his black cassock stood Father Rye.

As he saw me he smiled and snapped off his black-rimmed glasses.

'Well, John Rowland – what can I do for you this morning?'

I looked at him. I couldn't help feeling that he was like some tropical bird which had suddenly been turned into an everyday crow. Was this the man who had just murmured the divine words? Who minutes ago had taken the bread and the wine and trans-substantiated them into the body and blood of Christ?

'Well?' said Father Rye. As he spoke he rubbed the lenses of his glasses on the dark sleeve of his cassock.

I felt ashamed of my thoughts. To think like that about a priest! A man chosen by God! How terrible!

'I have been given a vocation,' I blurted out.

'I hope it is so,' said the priest, 'and I pray constantly for you. I ask God for one priest from this parish. But you haven't heard anything from the colleges – have you?'

'Yes,' I said, 'Saint Paul's. They've taken me.'

'You passed the exam?'

'Yes,' I said, but I wasn't really sure. I suspected that the rector of Saint Paul's in a moment of union with God had been ordered to ignore my examination results. I believed that God could intervene at any point in the daily motion of life and frequently did so.

'And you have a letter?'

'It came this morning.'

Father Rye made a swift sign of the cross and flung out both his arms, fingers splayed. I felt he was about to embrace me and self-consciously held myself still. But far from hugging me, he slapped his hands together, crossed his thumbs and lifting his head to the ceiling, murmured, 'Deo Gratias!'

'And now,' he said, looking at me, 'to business. Where's the letter?'

'At home,' I said.

'And what are the fees? They're important. Do you remember?'

'I don't know.'

'Don't know? Didn't you read the letter?'

'No, Father, there wasn't time. We were so excited you see.'

'But you are sure there was a letter?'

'Yes, Father.'

'I see. Well, I'll have to see your parents about that, won't I? We might have to arrange something there. A Sunday collection or something.'

'Yes, Father,' I said, barely understanding.

'The best thing,' said Father Rye, 'is for me to discuss these things with your parents. Do you think they could come and see me tonight?'

'My mother could,' I said, thinking it was best to leave my father out of it.

'And your father?' said Father Rye. 'I would like to see him too. I know he must be feeling proud of you. Especially as he's a convert. Could you ask them to come about eight? Oh – and one more thing – remind me, John, to announce the news in the notices on Sunday won't you? And there's something else. I must write to the Bishop to let him know. He has been so worried about the recent drop in vocations in our diocese.'

I cycled home slowly, feeling important. The Bishop was going to hear of me. My vocation was going to be announced from the pulpit. I was going to be a priest of God.

Deo Gratias!

IV

It was a wet morning. Miss Jenkins had told us to stay in. I sat on the window sill, still clutching an icy bottle of milk and slowly sucking up the delicious cold milk. Outside the rain plopped into the puddles. I could see Chris Edwards and John Parker with their navy gaberdines draped over their heads splashing each other. They never listened to what Miss Jenkins said. Chris was thrashing the puddles with a pole which he had pulled from Father Rye's garden while John was running round hurling handfuls of tiny stones which he kept scooping up from the playground. The rest of us were inside. Sally Abrahams was sitting on the desk nearest to me. She was pulling a pink wad of gum through her teeth, stretching it as far as she could and then slowly chewing it back again. By her stood her bottle of milk, the straws were bent and inside the milk had been all foamed up.

I was in love with Sally. At Christmas I had made her a card. I had made a star with silver tinsel – but I had never sent it. And one day on the way back from school I had chalked a red heart on Staple Road Bridge and then I had put an arrow through it and written Sally's name.

Suddenly Sally slid off her desk and came and stood by the window.

'Want a bit of gum?' she said.

'Got a bit to spare?' I said.

'I got a gob-stopper,' she said.

As she spoke Sally stuck out one of her inkblue fingers and began to draw on one of the steamy window panes.

'Okay,' I said.

'Don't let my sis know,' she said.

'Not if you don't want me to,' I said.

'Wait a sec then.'

I waited as Sally's blue finger moved across the window pane. She had drawn a boy in short trousers with a brush of hair on his head. She was now busily dotting a galaxy of freckles across the nose.

'Who's that?' she said, pulling out her purse from the top of her navy knickers.

'I don't know,' I said, but I hoped it was me.

'Can't you guess by all them funny spots?' She pulled back the zip on her purse and handed me a purple gobstopper. It was like a large shiny marble.

'No, I can't tell.'

I pushed the ball of gum into my mouth.

'You have *one* guess,' she said.

'Wait a jiff,' I said.

I wet the tip of my first finger and taking the next pane of glass drew a large face. I scribbled the hair in, drew straight lines for the eyes and nose, and then I drew a large 'O'-shaped mouth filling it with triangular teeth.

'It's a crocodile!' shouted Sally.

'Wait!' I shouted.

'It's you at the dentist – with a gobstopper – and it won't come out.'

I didn't answer. Instead I quickly drew in the last clue. I drew a blob of gum on the pinnacle of the largest triangle and then a hand stretching it out so that it looked like a sagging telegraph wire.

'That's me!' shouted Sally.

Her immediate act of recognition gave me confidence.

'And that,' I said, pointing to the little boy with freckles, 'is me!'

''Course it is!' said Sally.

Then Miss Jenkins came in ringing the handbell. We ran to put our bottles back in the crate.

'Hurry up! Hurry up!' said Miss Jenkins.

We scampered back to our desks.

'Come along now. Desk tops down. In your chairs. Ronald? Jane? Backs straight! Arms folded!'

Sally looked at me and winked. She pointed to our drawings. Ann whispered:

'Let's see how long they last.'

'Okay,' I said.

We were now sitting silently in our desks. Our backs were straight. Our arms were folded. Our eyes were staring straight into Miss Jenkins. I had already pulled out the large sticky gobstopper and wrapped it in my handkerchief.

Suddenly the large varnished door creaked open behind us.

'Good morning boys and girls.'

We recognized the voice at once and chanted:

'Good morning Father Rye!' Though we still remained staring at Miss Jenkins.

'And how are things this morning?'

As Father Rye made his way to the front of the classroom his black cassock brushed over my desk.

'As well as we can expect, Father,' said Miss Jenkins as her finger swept into the air and pointed pistol-like at Sally.

'Stand up!'

We all looked at Sally as she clambered to her feet. Her cheeks were scarlet, her eyes wet with some unknown pain.

'Well, child? What have you to say for yourself?'

'Nothing, Miss.'

'What were you chewing?'

'Nothing, Miss.'

'I've told you before, chewing is a loathsome habit. Loathsome! And it's perfectly disgusting when a priest is in the room. Come here at once and throw it into the bin.'

Sally walked out to the bin which always stood under Miss Jenkins's desk. And there she stood—staring into it.

'Well, go on then,' shrieked Miss Jenkins. 'It's wrong to draw attention to yourself like this.'

Father Rye, tactfully waiting for the episode to end, stood near the window. He was looking at our drawings, and I noticed he was shaking his head as if with disapproval. He seemed to be looking down upon them from some infinite height of wisdom and knowledge.

Well, I thought to myself, as I watched him, perhaps the drawings were rather silly. Certainly it wasn't the same as holding out one's hands and chanting 'Gloria in Excelsis Deo'. Nor was it like being crucified and then rising from the dead. What place, I wondered, could lolling in the window, drawing faces and chewing gum have in the eternal order of things?

Poor Sally was still staring into the bin.

'Please, Miss,' she was saying, 'I can't spit it out.'

'Please,' said Miss Jenkins, 'don't keep Father Rye waiting any longer.'

At the mention of his name Father Rye swished to the centre of the room and smiled at Miss Jenkins. He beckoned Sally to her place.

'Please, Father,' said Sally, in a low appealing voice, 'I can't spit it out 'cause I swallowed it.'

'Very well, my child,' said Father Rye, as if he had just heard the child's confession and was about to give a penance. 'Now, sit down and never do it again.'

He then raised his voice and spoke to all of us.

'I want you to listen carefully. I have great news for you. It concerns a vocation among you. Now I wonder how many of you know what a vocation is?'

He paused for a moment. I could see John Parker flicking quickly through the little red catechism which he kept under his desk. The right answer to Father Rye's questions often brought money.

Others were waving their hands frantically in the air.

Miss Jenkins now sat by the window. She wasn't paying much attention to us. She was busily cleaning the window panes with the palm of her hand. Sally's drawing had already disappeared.

'Well,' continued Father Rye, 'it's not a catechism lesson – so I won't ask you for the answer.' Rows of hands wilted in the air. John Parker sighed heavily and closed his catechism. The class was disappointed. The catechism lesson was the best lesson of the week. One afternoon, John Parker had earned himself half a crown.

'A vocation, you see,' said Father Rye, disregarding the class's disappointment, 'is a divine calling to be a priest. It is therefore the greatest calling there is. And a little school like this can consider itself blessed if it has one vocation every fifty years. Well, children, I will not keep you waiting any longer. The great news is this. John Rowland has been called by God to be a priest. Next term, when many of you will be working hard at the 11-plus, John will be off to Saint Paul's College for early vocations. I think we should first show our appreciation by clapping.'

Father Rye began to methodically clap his hands. Miss Jenkins followed. And then the children. The clapping thundered in my ears. Was I meant to clap or not? Was the clapping for me? Or for God? I felt very confused. I looked down at my desk, desperately waiting for it to end.

'And now,' said Father Rye, 'let us pray. Our Father—'

We stood up. We joined our hands and the clapping now gave way to chanting.

'Our Father—'

'Who art in Heaven—'

'Who art in Heaven—'

A.E.—6*

Unlike the rest of the class I merely mumbled the words. For the first time in my life I felt unreal, insubstantial, shadowy. Who was I? What was my vocation? Where was I going? What would happen to me?

'Thy Kingdom come—'

'Thy Kingdom come—'

'Thy will be done—'

'Thy will be done—'

Soon I would leave the school. Leave Sally. Leave home. Leave all the people I had ever known.

'On earth as it is in Heaven—'

'On earth as it is in Heaven—'

And what would become of me?

And where would this divine calling take me?

V

In the orange glow of the boiler my father's overalls drowsed like something half living. We were sitting round the table, my mother carving thick slices of crusty bread, my father daubing lumps of butter across them. Against the sweet butter the charred crusts tasted bitter and burnt. Steam spurted from the kettle's spout and drifted cloudlike below the flaking ceiling. Large drops of water sagged from the metal pipes but mysteriously never seemed to fall. My father, sleeves rolled up, shirt tails over his trousers, was busily talking, not to one of us but to a group of fellow gamblers who huddled in the dim corners of the room.

'*Black Boy* – I'm telling you. A dead cert. All the way. And there's a pile to be made by anyone who's got the sense. It's not the favourite – but never you mind about that. What I say is hot from the horse's mouth. You mark my words: *Black Boy*.'

'And you backed it?' said my mother.

'Course I backed it.'

'How much?' said my mother.

'Enough,' said my father, who never divulged any precise information about his gambling. '*And a bit more.*'

'We're still waiting for one of your winners,' said my mother.

'Ah – but this one's different. I've got this feeling. I know it in here.' My father butted his chest several times with the yellow handle of the butter knife. 'You see, I know it's a bloody certainty.

Be daft to let it go. Let my mates have the profits – and none myself. Well, that would be like suicide!'

'I suppose it would,' said my mother, indulgently – for she had her own reasons for wanting to keep my father purring.

'Well,' said my father, 'it's got to come my way one day. So much is as bright as sunlight.'

My brother and I had heard my father talk like this many times before. Except on Sundays, it was the daily teatime conversation. Yet we had little understanding of what my father was talking about. What did *Black Boy* or *Runaway* or *Darling Boy* refer to? To us they were dark beings whose names were tabulated on the back page of the daily paper and who every day (except Sunday) fatally lured my father forward only to betray him bitterly.

'When will you know?' said my mother.

'Tonight if I drop in the club sometime. And I'll buy a round of drinks. And tomorrow I'll buy you whatever you want.'

My mother laughed. But gently.

'I will. I will. Whatever you want.'

'Well,' she said, 'you have somewhere to go before then.'

'Have I?'

'With me. We've been invited to the presbytery.'

'Oh! What's all this?'

My father looked at me, his forehead rippling with frowns.

'Father Rye wants to see us about the letter,' said my mother.

'Oh, he does, does he?'

'At eight o'clock.'

'Well, we'll see about that.'

My mother persisted.

'I would like you,' she said, 'to wear your brown jacket. I mean, it's not like nipping down to the club is it? And your dark brown shoes which I've given a polish.'

'I said I'd see about it,' said my father, resisting.

'I've brushed your coat. It's on a hanger in the hall. And I'm sure Father Rye won't be long in saying what he's got to say, and then –' said my mother, 'you can drop in the club and see the results.'

'Well, we'll see. We'll see.'

My mother knew the art of persuasion. She said no more to my father. She turned to Martin and asked him about his Latin test. Then she began to clear the table. And, I remember, as she did so, she quietly hummed to herself.

VI

I woke up. It was dark. Outside I could hear the wind beating rain against the window. On the other side of the room I could hear Martin breathing, breathing deeply. And I could hear another sound. What was it? Was it the surge of the sea carried inland on the rough spikes of the wind? I sat up to listen. I could now see a rim of yellowish light issuing from under the door of my parents' bedroom. So they were back from the presbytery and the club!

Now I could hear my father's voice, unusually soft and consoling.

'Don't cry! Don't cry any more! There's no need!'

The sobbing subsided. Started again. Again, subsided.

'Look,' came my father's voice, 'if you really want him to go – well he can.'

'But it isn't just me who wants him to go,' sighed my mother.

'Well, Father Rye then.'

'And it's not just Father Rye either. Can't you see it is God who wants it? It's God who is calling him.'

'That's as may be,' said my father.

'That's because you don't believe. If you did believe you'd want John to go.'

'All I want,' said my father, 'is for him to wait. Let him wait. Let him see what he feels like at twenty.'

'Twenty!' said my mother. 'But he may have lost his calling by then! And then who'll be to blame? It will be *my* fault. *My* failing. And God will know and –'

My mother paused ominously before the black weight of her fears –

'And He might never forgive me. Never. Never forgive me.'

At this my mother began sobbing again and I could now hear my father pacing across their bedroom, backwards and forwards. Backwards and forwards. On the other side of the room I suddenly saw the dark outline of Martin lurching up in his bed.

Then my mother began talking.

'Well anyway,' she said, 'he's got a place at Saint Paul's. And the congregation are going to collect money for him. Everybody believes in him – except you. And what do you want him to do? What else is there he can do?'

'He can go to the Secondary Modern up the road.'

'You want him to go *there*?'

'Well that's where most lads go, isn't it?'

'Most lads! But John is *ours*. What an ambition for your own son! To want him to go to that rowdy school!'

'It's the sort of school I went to.'

'But it's not the sort of school John is going to. *I* am going to let him go to the seminary. *I* am giving him up to God. *I* am making the sacrifice.'

'Sacrifice? Giving him up? I think you enjoy the whole bloody thing.'

I could now hear my mother crying bitterly and my father's footsteps as he again padded like some chained and helpless beast across his cage.

Martin looked across at me.

'It's all your fault,' he said.

'What is?' I said.

'What they're arguing about.'

I waited, surprised and hurt that my brother should blame me.

'You're just doing it, aren't you – because you can't get into Grammar School? You have to create all this stuff about a vocation instead. You're jealous. That's what! Jealous!'

I resisted what Martin said with my whole being.

'You're wrong,' I said. 'Wrong. If we feel called by God, if we know we have something we must do, then we must do it. When Christ was found teaching in the temple at an early age he wasn't sorry that he had upset his mother and father, was he? He had to do it. He was *called* to do it.'

I looked across at my brother. I could see his head slumped into the pillow. He was breathing deeply. He had heard nothing of what I said.

My parents were talking again. But I couldn't bear to listen to them. I lay back in my bed longing to fall asleep.

Then I could see above me a boulder, falling, falling. Although it was much wider than my arms and altogether bigger than me, I managed to catch it and hold it. But then I was too afraid to let go of it, so that wherever I went, whatever I did, I was obliged to heave this burden with me.

I fell in a restless sleep until morning.

VII

Recently I found the following letter in a box of assortments in the attic of my old bedroom. There was no date on the letter, but

I remember writing it at some point in the middle of my first term at Saint Paul's College.

Dear Mother and Father,

How can I tell you about this place? It is – if you can understand what I mean – like a silent station. We must do everything on time but we are seldom allowed to talk. We are not allowed to talk in the dormitory or on the stairs or at meals or in the study or in the class-rooms.

We get up each morning at seven and have Morning Prayers and Mass. We then do manual labour. At quarter to nine we eat breakfast in silence. Then come lessons. During dinner a boy reads in Latin from the rostrum – and if he doesn't read it well enough the rector rings a bell and makes him read it again and again. After dinner we are allowed to talk for half-an-hour. During the afternoon we have more lessons, manual labour, and tea – three slices of bread. In the evening we study in the large hall. We are not allowed to talk there and prefects sit all round the room in high desks and report us when they wish to the Master of Discipline. At seven thirty a bell rings and we make our way to the chapel for rosary. We file out of the chapel into the dining hall for supper where a prefect reads to us from *The Life of Cardinal Vaughan*. After supper we have recreation – I often play table-tennis – but we are not allowed to keep playing with the same person. Then, at the end of the day, we have night prayers and night study. I am so tired when we get to the dormitory I fall asleep straight away, only the last five nights one of the boys has been crying, keeping most of us awake. He says he wants to return home but the rector says he must stay for at least another year to be sure of God's will.

Last night I dreamt that there had been a drought and that the world had shrivelled and dried up. Where there had been rivers and oceans there was now only dry deserts cracked like jigsaw puzzles.

I am posting this letter secretly in the village as the rector has asked me not to tell you these things when we write our Sunday letters, I hope nobody will find out. Please do not mention this letter when you write back.

The seminary is testing my vocation. I will not give in. We shouldn't cry at night but listen in the dark to what God has to say to us.

I think of you nearly all the time.

John

I have read the letter many times.

Did I write it?

Did I really go to the seminary?

I sit in my study listening to the wind as it somersaults over the fields. And the past seems never to have been.

And yet I know if I am to move forwards I must possess myself. And to possess myself I must scan backwards.

What am I to become?

What am I to do with my life, my time?

I look back to that day when the letter arrived. Beneath the words and gestures, beneath the hopes and fantasies, my life is hidden. There I must look.

I will hold all that I can.

I will cup my hands tightly together. I will allow nothing to dribble through my fingers.

V Ten Autobiographical Poems

The Retreat

Happy those early dayes! when I
Shin'd in my Angell-infancy.
Before I understood this place
Appointed for my second race,
Or taught my soul to fancy ought
But a white, Celestiall thought;
When yet I had not walkt above
A mile, or two, from my first love,
And looking back (at that short space,)
Could see a glimpse of his bright-face;
When on some *gilded Cloud*, or *flowre*
My gazing soul would dwell an houre,
And in those weaker glories spy
Some shadows of eternity;
Before I taught my tongue to wound
My Conscience with a sinfull sound,
Or had the black art to dispence
A sevrall sinne to ev'ry sence,
But felt through all this fleshly dresse
Bright shootes of everlastingnesse.

O how I long to travell back
And tread again that ancient track!
That I might once more reach that plaine,
Where first I left my glorious traine,
From whence th'Inlightned spirit sees
That shady City of Palme trees;
But (ah!) my soul with too much stay
Is drunk and staggers in the way.

Some men a forward motion love,
But I by backward steps would move,
And when this dust falls to the urn
In that state I came return.

HENRY VAUGHAN

Wonder

How like an Angel came I down!
How bright are all things here!
When first among His works I did appear
O how their glory me did crown!
The world resembled His Eternity
In which my soul did walk;
And every thing that I did see
Did with me talk.

The skies in their magnificence,
The lively, lovely air,
Oh how divine, how soft, how sweet, how fair!
The stars did entertain my sense,
And all the works of God so bright and pure,
So rich and great did seem,
As if they ever must endure
In my esteem.

A native health and innocence
Within my bones did grow,
And while my God did all his Glories show,
I felt a vigour in my sense
That was all Spirit. I within did flow
With seas of life, like wine;
I nothing in the world did know
But 'twas divine.

Harsh ragged objects were concealed,
Oppressions, tears and cries,
Sins, griefs, complaints, dissensions, weeping eyes
Were hid, and only things revealed

Which heavenly Spirits and the Angels prize.
The state of Innocence
And bliss, not trades and poverties,
Did fill my sense.

The streets were paved with golden stones,
The boys and girls were mine,
Oh how did all their lovely faces shine!
The sons of men were holy ones,
In joy and beauty they appeared to me,
And every thing which here I found,
While like an Angel I did see,
Adorned the ground.

Rich diamond and pearl and gold
In every place was seen;
Rare splendours, yellow, blue, red, white and green,
Mine eyes did everywhere behold.
Great wonders clothed with glory did appear,
Amazement was my bliss,
That and my wealth was everywhere;
No joy to this!

Cursed and devised proprieties,
With envy, avarice
And fraud, those fiends that spoil even Paradise,
Flew from the splendour of mine eyes,
And so did hedges, ditches, limits, bounds,
I dreamed not aught of those,
But wandered over all men's grounds,
And found repose.

Proprieties themselves were mine,
And hedges ornaments;
Walls, boxes, coffers, and their rich contents
Did not divide my joys, but all combine.
Clothes, ribbons, jewels, laces, I esteemed
My joys by others worn:
For me they all to wear them seemed
When I was born.

THOMAS TRAHERNE

The Ecchoing Green

The Sun does arise,
And make happy the skies;
The merry bells ring
To welcome the Spring;
The skylark and thrush,
The birds of the bush,
Sing louder around
To the bells' chearful sound
While our sports shall be seen
On the Ecchoing Green.

Old John, with white hair,
Does laugh away care,
Sitting under the oak,
Among the old folk.
They laugh at our play,
And soon they all say:
'Such, such were the joys
'When we all, girls & boys,
'In our youth time were seen
'On the Ecchoing Green.'

Till the little ones, weary,
No more can be merry;
The sun does descend,
And our sports have an end.
Round the laps of their mothers
Many sisters and brothers,
Like birds in their nest,
Are ready for rest,
And sport no more seen
On the darkening green.

WILLIAM BLAKE

Frost at Midnight

The Frost performs its secret ministry,
Unhelped by any wind. The owlet's cry
Came loud – and hark, again! loud as before.
The inmates of my cottage, all at rest,
Have left me to that solitude, which suits
Abstruser musings: save that at my side
My cradled infant slumbers peacefully.
'Tis calm indeed! so calm, that it disturbs
And vexes meditation with its strange
And extreme silentness. Sea, hill, and wood,
This populous village! Sea, and hill, and wood,
With all the numberless goings-on of life,
Inaudible as dreams! the thin blue flame
Lies on my low-burnt fire, and quivers not;
Only that film, which fluttered on the grate,
Still flutters there, the sole unquiet thing.
Methinks, its motion in this hush of nature
Gives it dim sympathies with me who live,
Making it a companionable form,
Whose puny flaps and freaks the idling Spirit
By its own moods interprets, every where
Echo or mirror seeking of itself,
And makes a toy of Thought.
                         But O! how oft,
How oft, at school, with most believing mind,
Presageful, have I gazed upon the bars,
To watch that fluttering *stranger*! and as oft
With unclosed lids, already had I dreamt
Of my sweet birth-place, and the old church-tower,
Whose bells, the poor man's only music, rang
From morn to evening, all the hot Fair-day,
So sweetly, that they stirred and haunted me
With a wild pleasure, falling on mine ear
Most like articulate sounds of things to come!
So gazed I, till the soothing things, I dreamt,
Lulled me to sleep, and sleep prolonged my dreams!
And so I brooded all the following morn,
Awed by the stern preceptor's face, mine eye
Fixed with mock study on my swimming book:

Save if the door half opened, and I snatched
A hasty glance, and still my heart leaped up,
For still I hoped to see the *stranger*'s face,
Townsman, or aunt, or sister more beloved,
My play-mate when we both were clothed alike!

Dear Babe, that sleepest cradled by my side,
Whose gentle breathings, heard in this deep calm,
Fill up the interspersed vacancies
And momentary pauses of the thought!
My babe so beautiful! it thrills my heart
With tender gladness, thus to look at thee
And think that thou shalt learn far other lore,
And in far other scenes! For I was reared
In the great city, pent 'mid cloisters dim,
And saw nought lovely but the sky and stars.
But *thou*, my babe! shalt wander like a breeze
By lakes and sandy shores, beneath the crags
Of ancient mountain, and beneath the clouds,
Which image in their bulk both lakes and shores
And mountain crags: so shalt thou see and hear
The lovely shapes and sounds intelligible
Of that eternal language, which thy God
Utters, who from eternity doth teach
Himself in all, and all things in himself.
Great Universal Teacher! he shall mould
Thy spirit, and by giving, make it ask.

Therefore all seasons shall be sweet to thee,
Whether the summer clothe the general earth
With greenness, or the redbreast sit and sing
Betwixt the tufts of snow on the bare branch
Of mossy apple-tree, while the nigh thatch
Smokes in the sun-thaw; whether the eave-drops fall
Heard only in the trances of the blast,
Or if the secret ministry of frost
Shall hang them up in silent icicles,
    Quietly shining to the quiet Moon.

S. T. COLERIDGE

To Margaret

Margarét, are you grieving
Over Goldengrove unleaving?
Leaves, like the things of man, you
With your fresh thoughts care for, can you?
Ah! as the heart grows older
It will come to such sights colder
By and by, nor spare a sigh
Though worlds of wanwood leafmeal lie;
And yet you will weep and know why.
Now no matter, child, the name:
Sorrow's springs are the same.
Nor mouth had, no nor mind, expressed
What heart heard of, ghost guessed:
It is the blight man was born for,
It is Margaret you mourn for.

GERARD MANLEY HOPKINS

Child on Top of a Greenhouse

The wind billowing out the seat of my britches,
My feet crackling splinters of glass and dried putty,
The half-grown chrysanthemums staring up like
    accusers,
Up through the streaked glass, flashing with sunlight,
A few white clouds all rushing eastwards
A line of elms plunging and tossing like horses,
And everyone, everyone pointing up and shouting.

THEODORE ROETHKE

Fern Hill

Now as I was young and easy under the apple boughs
About the lilting house and happy as the grass was
    green,

The night above the dingle starry,
    Time let me hail and climb
  Golden in the heydays of his eyes,
And honoured among wagons I was prince of the
        apple towns
And once below a time I lordly had the trees and leaves
    Trail with daisies and barley
  Down the rivers of the windfall light.

And as I was green and carefree, famous among the
    barns
About the happy yard and singing as the farm was
    home,
  In the sun that is young once only,
    Time let me play and be
  Golden in the mercy of his means,
And green and golden I was huntsman and herdsman,
    the calves
Sang to my horn, the foxes on the hills barked clear
    and cold,
    And the sabbath rang slowly
  In the pebbles of the holy streams.

All the sun long it was running, it was lovely, the hay-
Fields high as the house, the tunes from the chimneys,
    it was air
  And playing, lovely and watery
    And fire green as grass.
  And nightly under the simple stars
As I rode to sleep the owls were bearing the farm away,
All the moon long I heard, blessed among stables,
    the nightjars
    Flying with the ricks, and horses
      Flashing into the dark.

And then to awake, and the farm, like a wanderer
    white
With the dew, come back, the cock on his shoulder: it
    was all
  Shining, it was Adam and maiden,
    The sky gathered again

And the sun grew round that very day.
So it must have been after the birth of the simple light
In the first, spinning place, the spellbound horses
        walking warm
    Out of the whinnying green stable
        On to the fields of praise.

And honoured among foxes and pheasants by the gay
        house
Under the new-made clouds and happy as the heart
        was long
    In the sun born over and over,
        I ran my heedless ways,
        My wishes raced through the house-high hay
And nothing I cared, at my sky blue trades, that time
        allows
In all his tuneful turning so few and such morning
        songs
    Before the children green and golden
        Follow him out of grace.

Nothing I cared, in the lamb white days, that time
        would take me
Up to the swallow-thronged loft by the shadow of my
        hand,
    In the moon that is always rising,
        Nor that riding to sleep
    I should hear him fly with the high fields
And wake to the farm forever fled from the childless
        land.
Oh as I was young and easy in the mercy of his means,
    Time held me green and dying
    Though I sang in my chains like the sea.

DYLAN THOMAS

Piano

Softly, in the dusk, a woman is singing to me;
Taking me back down the vista of years, till I see
A child sitting under the piano, in the boom of the
    tingling strings
And pressing the small, poised feet of a mother who
    smiles as she sings.

In spite of myself, the insidious mastery of song
Betrays me back, till the heart of me weeps to belong
To the old Sunday evenings at home, with winter
    outside
And hymns in the cosy parlour, the tinkling piano our
    guide.

So now it is vain for the singer to burst into clamour
With the great black piano appassionato. The glamour
Of childish days is upon me, my manhood is cast
Down in the flood of remembrance, I weep like a child
    for the past.

D. H. LAWRENCE

Old Man

Old Man, or Lad's-love, in the name there's nothing
To one that knows not Lad's-love, or Old Man,
The hoar-green feathery herb, almost a tree,
Growing with rosemary and lavender.
Even to one that knows it well, the names
Half decorate, half perplex, the thing it is:
At least, what that is clings not to the names
In spite of time. And yet I like the names.

The herb itself I like not, but for certain
I love it, as some day the child will love it
Who plucks a feather from the door-side bush
Whenever she goes in or out of the house.
Often she waits there, snipping the tips and shrivelling
The shreds at last on to the path, perhaps
Thinking, perhaps of nothing, till she sniffs
Her fingers and runs off. The bush is still
But half as tall as she, though it is as old;
So well she clips it. Not a word she says;
And I can only wonder how much herafter
She will remember, with that bitter scent,
Of garden rows, and ancient damson trees
Topping a hedge, a bent path to a door,
A low thick bush beside the door, and me
Forbidding her to pick.

                              As for myself,
Where first I met the bitter scent is lost.
I too, often shrivel the grey shreds,
Sniff them and think and sniff again and try
Once more to think what it is I am remembering,
Always in vain. I cannot like the scent
Yet I would rather give up others more sweet,
With no meaning, than this bitter one.

I have mislaid the key. I sniff the spray
And think of nothing; I see and I hear nothing;
Yet seem, too, to be listening, lying in wait
For what I should, yet never can, remember:

No garden appears, no path, no hoar green-bush
Of Lad's-love, or Old Man, no child beside,
Neither father nor mother, nor any playmate;
Only an avenue, dark, nameless, without end.

EDWARD THOMAS

from *Burnt Norton*

Time present and time past
Are both perhaps present in time future,
And time future contained in time past.
If all time is eternally present
All time is unredeemable.
What might have been is an abstraction
Remaining a perpetual possibility
Only in a world of speculation.
What might have been and what has been
Point to one end, which is always present.
Footfalls echo in the memory
Down the passage which we did not take
Towards the door we never opened
Into the rose-garden. My words echo
Thus, in your mind.

But to what purpose
Disturbing the dust on a bowl of rose-leaves
I do not know.

Other echoes
Inhabit the garden. Shall we follow?
Quick, said the bird, find them, find them,
Round the corner. Through the first gate,
Into our first world, shall we follow
The deception of the thrush? Into our first world.
There they were, dignified, invisible,
Moving without pressure, over the dead leaves,
In the autumn heat, through the vibrant air,

And the bird called, in response to
The unheard music hidden in the shrubbery,
And the unseen eyebeam crossed, for the roses
Had the look of flowers that are looked at.
There they were as our guests, accepted and accepting.
So we moved, and they, in a formal pattern,
Along the empty alley, into the box circle,
To look down into the drained pool.
Dry the pool, dry concrete, brown edged,
And the pool was filled with water out of sunlight,
And the lotos rose, quietly, quietly
The surface glittered out of heart of light,
And they were behind us, reflected in the pool.
Then a cloud passed, and the pool was empty.
Go, said the bird, for the leaves were full of children,
Hidden excitedly, containing laughter.
Go, go, go, said the bird: human kind
Cannot bear very much reality.
Time past and time future
What might have been and what has been
Point to one end, which is always present.

T. S. ELIOT

VI Bibliography

1. On Autobiography

Roy Pascal: *Design and Truth in Autobiography* (RKP)

2. On Existentialism

William Barrett: *Irrational Man* (HEB)
Martin Buber: *Between Man and Man* (Fontana)
Hazel Barnes: *An Existentialist Ethics* (Wildwood House)
Roger Poole: *Towards Deep Subjectivity* (Allen Lane, Penguin Press)

3. On Psychotherapy and Education

Rollo May: *Love and Will* (Souvenir Press)
David Holbrook: *Human Hope and The Death Instinct* (Pergamon)
E. K. Ledermann: *Existential Neurosis* (Butterworth)
Marjorie Hourd: *Relationship in Learning* (HEB)
R. D. Laing: *The Divided Self* (Penguin)
D. W. Winnicott: *Playing and Reality* (Tavistock)
Erik Erikson: *Childhood and Society* (Penguin)
Victor Frankl: *Psychotherapy and Existentialism* (Penguin)
                The Doctor and the Soul (Penguin)

4. Other Autobiographies

Anthony Trollope: *An Autobiography* (Fontana)
Samuel Butler: *The Way of All Flesh*
John Ruskin: *Praeterita*
Beatrice Webb: *My Apprenticeship*

Flora Thompson: *Lark Rise to Candleford* (OUP)
        Still Glides the Stream
Edwin Muir: *An Autobiography*
W. B. Yeats: *Autobiographies* (Macmillan)
Tolstoy: *Childhood, Boyhood, Youth* (Penguin)
Yevtushenko: *A Precocious Autobiography* (Collins and Harvill Press)
Sartre: *Words* (Penguin)

5. *Autobiographical Novels*

James Joyce: *Portrait of the Artist as a Young Man*
D. H. Lawrence: *Sons and Lovers*

6. *Other Relevant Books*

Peter Brown: *Augustine of Hippo* (Faber)
George Woodcock: *The Stream and the Source :* The Life of Herbert Read
    (Faber)
Graham Greene: *The Lost Childhood and Other Essays* (Penguin)
Peter Coveney: *The Image of Childhood* (Peregrine)
Ronald Sampson: *Equality and Power* (HEB)
William James: *The Varieties of Religious Experience*
Herbert Read: *Icon and Idea :* Chapter 6 (Faber)